I Might Be the Person
You Are Talking To

I Might Be the Person You Are Talking To

Short Plays from the Los Angeles Underground
Recent Work from Padua and Sharon's Farm

PADUA
PLAYWRIGHTS
PRODUCTION

Padua Playwrights Press, Los Angeles

Produced by Sideshow Media LLC, New York, NY

Editorial director: Dan Tucker
Cover design: Tung, Toronto
Interior template: CoDe. New York Inc., Jenny 8 del Corte Hirschfeld and
Mischa Leiner
Supervising Padua editor: Guy Zimmerman
Assistant Padua editor: Gray Palmer
Cover painting: "Flow," Courtesy of The Estate of James Doolin & Koplin Del
Rio Gallery, Culver City, CA

Guy Zimmerman
Padua Playwrights Productions
840 Micheltorena Street
Los Angeles CA 90026

Printed in the United States of America

Distributed in the United States and Canada by theater Communications Group,
520 Eighth Avenue, 24th Floor, New York, NY 10018-4156
ISBN: 978-0-9907256-1-9

Contents

Escaping Voices
New Plays from Ground Zero

by Guy Zimmerman

1. *Monstrous Hybrids*

The automotive dream of Los Angeles inverts the theatrical impulse, presenting a figure of pure speed and mobility. We no longer look across a magic line in the sand and say "over there can be anywhere and any time" but instead hit the ignition and lose ourselves in pure transversality—the anywhere of no place in particular at eighty miles per hour. To one degree or another the plays collected here make peace with this basic arrangement, trafficking in anomaly and drift, the hybrid and the transitory— they are dreams to be engaged with in the freakish state called rest, on-ramps to the forgotten realm of the virtual. They owe their existence to a marriage between two wildly different strata—the unique minds of individual American writers from a certain time and place on the one hand, and the fractured and chaotic semi-urban ground of Los Angeles on the other.

Historically speaking, the specific time frame covered by this collection (2003–2014) coincides with the arrival of the Anthropocene, the post-human figure of thought that acquired critical mass around the turn of the century. The weight of our cities, our buildings and roads, the way we have *mineralized* the surface of the planet, registered to geologists suddenly as an inde-pendent strata, exerting a unique, tectonic force on the geosphere. If the planet is becoming a global parking lot, Los Angeles occupies ground zero—it is the place where automotive travel first became the organizational principle of a new, semi-urban kind of city, the place where machines burning fossil fuels began altering the basic chemistry of the Earth in return for taking people to work and to the beach. As the planet continues to heat, species will die off, our own eventually as well. Earth will then spin in space, a dark cinder, for hundreds of thousands of years... until natural processes and complex assemblages of desire emerge again, crawling up out of the ooze. By some unforeseen metabolic process, carbon gets re-sequestered, green shoots of new plants burst through the roads and paved streets. Buildings crumble, topsoil returns... until finally, after millions of years, tectonic activity completes the burial of the Anthropocene. But this planetary mantle of concrete and asphalt and steel will live on as a geologic layer, a strata in the earth to be discovered by some future species of sentient beings and scrutinized for news of the long lost age of man.

Fortunately, Los Angeles has always arguably been a place people come in order to lose track of the future and also the past, embracing instead the kind of speculative and spectral subjectivity referred to by this volume's title—*I Might Be the Person You Are Talking To*. And then again I might be someone entirely different, someone not here, not now, a personage yet to be actualized out of the pure capacities of this time and place. This immanent mode of being is ideal for the Anthropocene. Since the birth of tragedy, after all, the stage has been a mechanism to draw collective attention to <record-scratch effect> and the animals? Fuck 'em. They're dying. Saying this, writing this, I feel myself choke on words. I don't want to use words anymore—they're really to blame for the fix we find ourselves in. I want to burn language with acids. Make sure it never comes back. On the other hand, I love words and live on words.

To address the question of what all this has to do with writing for the stage, allow me to restate the familiar Padua dictum—we develop playwrights, not plays—and point out its distinctly political nature. With only one exception I know of these plays arose free of the kind of careerist yuppie mindset—what novelist and critic Sarah Schulman calls the "gentrification of the mind"—in which notes are delivered as part of some entertainment industry paradigm. No self-anointed producers have leveraged their control over access to audiences to enforce some template of what a "good" play should be; here, for better or worse, the playwright enters into a direct and unmediated relationship to her audience, giving rise to singular new aesthetics by which to re-code our relations to each other in unforeseen ways. While it is easy to take this L.A. mode of work for granted, such freedom is, in my experience, entirely unique and to be highly valued.

Let me add that I'm using the term "Padua" to cover a broad and diverse community of artists influenced to one degree or another by Murray Mednick's Padua Hills Playwrights Festival/Workshop. An important offshoot of New York's Off-Off Broadway movement, the Festival ran from 1978 to 1995, and its influence was amplified in Los Angeles by the artistic activities of its main playwrights, most especially John Steppling. An original member of Padua, and the artistic director of several transformational new works theater collectives, Steppling has had a strong impact on most, if not all, of the playwrights collected here, myself included. As it happens three of these plays—by Boyd, Rossi and Jensen—first appeared under the banner of Steppling's *Gunfighter Nation*, the company he created during a recent two-year window (between 2011 and 2013) when he returned from Europe. While I did not produce these three plays—the playwrights have many other living connections to the broader community—I asked them to participate in the anthology, and these are the texts they sent to me.

All in all, this volume presents a community of writers and directors, a unique creative ecology, who have something worth saying about what it means to be alive in this place and time. These short plays give form to a certain kind of theater you could make in Los Angeles in the first decade of the 21st century. I asked Sharon Yablon to help me edit this volume because the long series of site-specific evenings she has staged represents the most energetic continuation of Padua's engagement with the semi-urban landscape of Los Angeles. One-off engagements presented free of charge, Sharon's Farm retains situationalist overtones, subtly re-coding the cityscape to liberative effect. Sharon speaks directly about those plays in her portion of the introduction, below; I'll focus on those printed here under the more general Padua banner.

2. *The Menagerie in a Line Up*
Sissy Boyd (*Sabine River*) and Susan Hayden (*The Advantages of a Steep Roof*) are both writers of importance in the extended Padua community. To general acclaim, Boyd has been composing her unique stage texts for the past two decades. We first worked together in the mid-90s as part of Steppling's previous company, Empire RedLip, and *Sabine River* continues the themes Boyd was exploring in her work at that time. Expressing the complex affects of dependency as it colors relationships between parents and children, Boyd has created a unique stage language that is both deeply poetic and deeply embodied, and she uses it to give voice to affective states of luminous calamity as singular as unicorns or griffins. Hayden, a poet and painter, was a student at the Festival back in the 80s. Among many other things, she has gone on to produce Library Girl, an important venue for new writing held regularly at the Miles Playhouse in Santa Monica. The Miles is

where I heard *Steep Roof* in an evening of short plays, and I immediately noticed the presence of the avant-garde, Padua aesthetic. There's a special feel for the sound of spoken dialogue, and this sound is dynamically linked to the singular shape the play will assume. *Steep Roof*, for example, manages to carry the defining qualities of a sputtering romance into the flickering, fire-like form of dialogue itself, Hayden's Cadillac-driving Sid confessing his love in the path of a bush fire.

Chris Rossi's play (*How to Talk to the Dead*) coalesces around the use of language in ritual and the incantatory power of words as part of the defining American trope of the con. Underscoring our complicity in the set of particular delusions that define our selves, *How to Talk to the Dead* dramatizes the closed, looping nature of the self foreclosing our efforts to find authentic connection. Marc Jensen contributes a play (*A Dead Horse Beaten*) defined in similar ways by a noir-ish preoccupation with sabotage and deception in the context of a decaying marriage. The playwright opens a door and listens, conveying insights about the kind of slow, mutually deadening entanglement defining an emblematic modern marriage.

Two of the other plays, *The Diagnosis* by Coleman Hough, and Heidi Darchuk's *Knots* were produced as a part of a workshop Hough and I ran in 2007. Like several other plays in this volume (*Pink*, *The Asia Campaign* and *Numerology*) *The Diagnosis* was inventively staged by the playwright at Jim Fittipaldi's legendary speakeasy on 6th Street, Bedlam, as a Padua/Sharon's Farm hybrid event. Hough had recently been diagnosed with Parkinson's, and the piece is a darkly humorous replaying of that shattering event. There's a kind of bracing absurdism at work in Hough's deadpan humor, drawing us close to the terrifying fragility of embodiment with a fatalistic equanimity. One of the highlights of Padua's collaboration with visual artists in 2008 (*A Thousand Words*), Darchuk's *Knots,* meanwhile, was inspired by the playwright's encounter with a haunting painting by Jett Jackson showing a woman's back lit up by nautical tattoos. Weaving imagery and facts gleaned from her conversations with the painter together with research into the craft of sailing and her own active imagination, Darchuk's play exudes a hybrid, mermaid charm. I loved how Gill Gayle staged the play, and how Darchuk managed to capture some of the main themes of our workshop, which that year had the Lacanian title *Desire and the Other.*

Three of the plays, Gray Palmer's *Plan B*, my own *Hello, Say* and Rachel Jendrzejewski's *Amber* were part of an experimental triptych Padua developed in 2012. In a series of conversations Palmer and I discussed the political implications of some of Gilles Deleuze and Felix Guattari's ideas in *A Thousand Plateaus* as they pertain to the looming environmental crises of our time, and a kind of politicized, post-human dream-play project involving human–bee interactions emerged. The triptych opens with Palmer's *Plan B* in which a disillusioned labor organizer, struggling with a misanthropic species of despair, dreams of being "abducted by a goddess." Drawing from the narrative techniques of ancient Greek novels and the work of the second century author Apuleius, *Plan B* collides labor politics with tropes out of the iconic sitcom "I Dream of Jeannie." Palmer's fictionalized labor organizer encounters in his basement an inter-species emissary, who invites him to abandon our doomed species. As the second entry in the trilogy, my own *Hello, Say* extends this dream of hybridized awarenesses into the terrain of noir. The dark and inhuman corporate executive is a stable of my work as a playwright, and in

Hello, Say the real-world machinations of a flamboyant (and probably murderous) executive recently in the news provided fuel for an exploration of an encounter in the Tibetan bardo with a bee-like hybrid creature. Gray and I commissioned Rachel Jendrzejewski to contribute a piece and *Amber* could not have been a stronger completion of this Deleuzian journey into an intensive realm. The two female figures in *Amber* manage to charm us in the direction of our own demise. Dancing out an otherworldly *mathesis* they have derived from the chemical nature of honey, these beings welcome us to a world in which a different species occupies the center of things, drawing the energies of our attention into projects we are not equipped to comprehend. Performed in a number of venues in Los Angeles, and then presented at the Society for Literature, Science and the Arts (SLSA) conference at Notre Dame, *The Hive* project remains an active engagement, and we are currently in conversation with several theaters nationwide.

Extending this new environmental focus, the anthology also includes my own play *Forget Me That Way* which was performed at a recent site-specific event in the Frog Town neighborhood of Atwater Village. Like *Hello, Say, Forget Me That Way* unfolds in a liminal space between life and death. This neo-Noh play dramatizes the torment a psychotic genetic engineer inflicts on the spirits of his ex-wife and her lover, with potentially dire consequences for the audience of the play. Juli Crockett's *Saint Simone*, meanwhile, is a brilliant fragment of a longer work dedicated to the remarkable World War II-era thinker Simone Weil. A gifted creative polymath, Crockett deconstructs the toxic mindset of two demented attorneys followed by a female chorus speaking for the saint-like Weil. While I'm intrigued to see how this piece evolves into a full evening of theater this excerpt should be staged as part of some evening of new short plays and I'm thrilled to have it in the anthology.

3. *Where to Listen From*

With a certain savagery the best of these plays seek to corrode our faith in simplistic solutions to our current slate of problems grounded in some version of common sense. Our "opponent" as we grapple with social and economic justice, global warming and species extinction uses paradox and contradiction to frustrate our efforts to find clarity. We therefore want to use the mechanisms of the stage to engage collectively in new ways, embracing the basic paradoxes of dramatic representation to come at these problems from new angles. We want to use theater to travel to the edge of the dark and listen there for new ideas about who we might be, and how we might find a way forward. Our future may be far different, better or worse, than the slow demise I describe above—it is impossible to know. In my fondest fantasies, we find a way to engage with the living systems of the planet in some new mode of exquisitely responsive species-wide dance, but I also believe its important for us to look at the darker possibilities without embellishment.

Entering Prison Area Do Not Pick Up Hitchhikers
Site-specific Theater in Los Angeles

by Sharon Yablon

I was very lucky that the Walt Disney Company granted me six weeks'
leave without pay from my administrative job so I could take the
summer Padua Hills Playwrights Program in 1993. Those days flew by
like a wonderful fever dream of writing, intellectual discussion,
learning how to stage site-specific plays, and apprenticing to such wildly
original playwrights as John O'Keefe. As his assistant, I got to witness
first hand his creation of a play of tormented sisters that he staged on a
grassy hill. I'll never forget seeing the image of the women at the top of
the hill for the first time in their billowy white dresses, and hearing his
crazy, exuberant language from the grass below. I had not considered
writing site-specific work before, but now I was hooked. Years later,
when I started Sharon's Farm, those first elements of excitement and
wonder remained with me as I drove around Los Angeles, falling in love
with potential sites for plays.

The plays included in this book are among the most exciting
pieces that I was able to stage over the years through Sharon's
Farm. They come from a very talented pool of playwrights, many
of whom I continue to collaborate with.

April Rouveyrol's two-character piece, *Shy,* explores the mystery of
memory in the particular dark way that April writes. It was the last
play of five staged at the top of Wattles Park one evening, after it
had cooled down. A girl sits amid ruins (where the park merges
with trails in the Hollywood Hills), vulnerable, as a man, eyes fixed

on her, descends from the hillside. We experience a dangerous dance between a girl and a seductive predator. The lyricism of the language suggests that we are seeing a reunion that is infused with the imagination and memory of a girl trying to make sense of her past. There is mystery about the man and what happened: did he go "straight from that tree in the park to doing something horrible?" "Adolescence came and went and you weren't there," the man says, hinting at innocence shattered. But maybe it's worth it, as he's someone "who electrifies every cell in your body and turns you from stone to liquid from a stranger to a lover." Wattles is my favorite park in L.A., its crumbling pillars and benches speak of a lost glamour. When non-audience members realized what we were doing, they often glanced our way, curious, and some even came near and watched. Wattles Park is a special place for me because I used to get stoned there with friends growing up. I'm sure I took more than one boy to make out there. But it also had a dark side, and I was attracted to that: I once saw two proud transvestites come out of the bushes (possibly after sex), and I would often see lone people who looked strung out. It's a Los Angeles "noir" park. The city's marginalized and uncelebrated folk are often those I am drawn to write about, and they seem to gravitate to Wattles Park. The boundary at the top of the park rambles off into the Hollywood Hills where there are still occasional satanic sacrifices, I hear. I call it a "hidden gem" of L.A.

Before my play *The Party* was produced by Padua at the Lillian Theater in Hollywood, it premiered in the lobby of a now defunct resident hotel on Hollywood Boulevard. A friend knew a woman who worked there, a large dominatrix with pink hair who could have passed for Divine's daughter, and when I ran the idea of doing short plays in the hotel by her, she answered me with a surly "Yeah." I remember encouraging her to do one of her sadistic performances in the hallway, but she declined (I think dominatrixes are used to making a lot of money). *The Party* started our afternoon and was performed in the lobby. During the performance (I couldn't have asked for anything better!), a drugged-out Jesus look-alike entered the hotel and walked directly through our "stage," recited some odd thoughts from his head and then disappeared into the creaky elevator that looked as if it went to Hades itself. We moved to the other floors, where first the audience encountered actor Tom Waldman in a long hallway doing a monologue I wrote (*Apartment 17*), about a man making crank phone calls. The audience lined the walls on both sides as Tom traipsed up and down the rotting rug. They were then split into groups and taken to different hotel rooms for plays, including one of Michael Farkash's, whose work unfortunately I wasn't able to secure for this anthology. Mike passed away about ten years ago, but he was a huge and prolific part of our scene; I like to describe his plays as strange, horrific, and funny. I love skanky hotels like this that are little slivers of Hell, and it was a treat for me to subject my audience to this "hotel of horrors." It was dark, smelled some, and the locals who lived there would make Diane Arbus proud!

When I learned that my parents were going to sell the house I grew up in, I knew I had to do a Farm there. Five plays were staged in the yard and pool area of my parents' Beverly Hills house. The audience sat on the grass for Bernard Goldberg's play, *The Virtue of Hospitality*, watching a man and woman on lounge chairs. These two are not a couple, and the man quickly engages the woman in conversation. I love the things that this play brings up: vacations and being a tourist, mysterious agendas, encounters with strangers. Does the man want to sleep with the woman ("I feel we understand each other, you and I. Your experience leaves you in search of the authentic. The authentic stands against a backdrop of stagnation.")? Or does he have philosophical troubles he needs to unload (don't we all)? He tells her a story about his nephew's stay with him and the demise of his wife (who turns into a pillar of salt), but he's not the only one revealing personal things; a waiter and waitress take turns intruding upon them, peppering the pair with details of their own lives. I am always interested in how a writer finds inspiration, and when I asked Bernard about this play he said, "I was told the play would take place near a pool, so I envisioned a man and a woman lying on lounge chairs. I had been to the Dead Sea a few years earlier and, as I remembered floating in the water, thought about Lot's wife, who was turned into a pillar of salt near the Dead Sea. I then thought of Lot and his uncle, Abraham, from *Genesis*, and that led to stories from the Talmud, all of which swirled about and developed into the relationship between the man and woman lying next to the pool." There is always a humor in Bernard's writing and something wonderfully Dada-esque at play. The plays then moved to the pool house, pool, and Jacuzzi, where the actors got in the water as the plays dictated. When I look back on that day, I also remember the late and great actor Rick Dean, who remains one of the most compelling people I have seen onstage. Behind the pool was the pool house, where my first boyfriend and I would sneak make-out sessions, where I did mushrooms, and where later I lived briefly after moving back to L.A. from San Francisco, at a crossroads in my life (if someone had told me I would be doing theater there someday I would have been very surprised). There were so many memories in that house, as childhood homes harbor. I know the audience enjoyed being in someone's private space to witness theater. Many of my plays are set in houses, which continue to hold so much fascination for me. All of our private dramas and tragedies are played out in them. When we move, the house becomes a blank slate, a *tabula rasa*, for its next "victims." Yet it's not blank, because every house has a history.

I had always wanted to do plays in an office, and my friend Andy arranged for us to do plays after hours in the Santa Monica tech office where he worked. Office workers, not knowing what to expect from "site-specific theater," gathered in the lobby for my play *The Interview,* in which a man in drag is interviewed by a senior staffer who may or may not be coming on to him. Just as had happened in the hotel lobby, a person having nothing to do with the play interrupted the action—in this case it was a confused UPS man making a delivery. The actors handled his entrance quite well, as they had been prepared to do, and the UPS man was a great addition to the piece. Later in the evening, the audience was led to the back part of the office for Kevin O'Sullivan's fever dream, *Snakes and Ladders.* A man in a suit, who is possibly trying to prepare for the end of his corporate reign, asks the other man, who appears to be homeless, "What's it like, to lose everything?" A loaded question indeed, especially for two people at opposite ends of the economic ladder. A gasoline can separates them; will the man in the suit dump it on the homeless man because he is afraid of him, or because he doesn't like his appearance? Will the homeless man take out his rage on the other man, the one percent? Or has he transcended those feelings somehow, having endured life in a hellish culture whose values reward bad behavior, worship physical beauty, and destroy the individual?

Like a loaded gun, the gasoline can creates a great tension for the audience. I loved how Kevin's play exposed the truths that hide underneath the veneer of offices and people. It was exciting to experience the raw theatricality of the language in the blandness of an office setting. Kevin has gone on to producing his own site-specific theater event in a bar, the wildly successful Pharmacy. Like houses, hotels, and other buildings, an office commands a particular story. In other words, the rules are different in all of these settings, and thus impact the stories. People may not realize it, but there are many possibilities an office offers for drama, whether it occurs during office hours or after.

Guy Zimmerman and Padua co-produced an evening of Sharon's Farm plays at the artist and downtown L.A. historian Jim Fittipaldi's two-story loft, Bedlam. Cheryl Slean's play *Numerology* opened the evening, and was set near the large metal doors of the loft. Two men and a woman encounter each other under mysterious circumstances. How did they get there, and where is "there"? The things they talk about are colored by the proximity of Los Angeles (acting, aging, addiction, narcissism, conformity, individuality— "madly defining themselves, madly jabbing finger to chest, but no one is even listening"—and obsession with health). There's anger in the words, a defiance and frustration about trying to live up to these ideals; L.A. is supposed to be laid back, but it's not. Trapped, looking for meaning, the characters throw words out at each other, until the end, when the doors open. They venture out tentatively; are they ready? Are they in L.A., and can they even get out? ("You think you got out of town two hours ago and you look around and for chrissake you're still in it.") There is a force propelling Cheryl's writing, you can feel her interesting mind at work, thinking and questioning, in her plays. Cheryl is a longtime student of Murray Mednick's and is highly attuned to the Padua aesthetic. She is truly one who visits the site first, and then writes the play from there, letting the place feed her imagination. After Cheryl's play, the audience moved into an upstairs room where an austere woman sat with a laptop in Hank Bunker's play, *The Asia Campaign*. I still remember that feeling of first peeking into the room, and seeing the actors already in character, as if it really were a private moment we were witnessing. There is a tense fragility in Hank's play that comes from watching people quietly suffering, trying to make sense of their pasts, of contemporary life, and absent children. The woman, Greever, engages in her computer interface, possibly to disappear from the pain and disappointments in her life. The man, Pronk, is nervous to see his teenage son, who has been away for six years. The last time Pronk saw his son he was a child. How crucial a window had he missed to bond with him? A nearby abstract painting serves as a sort of mirror: "What does the picture mean? Can you tell me? I'm sure it means that we're all lost in a godless void. Isn't that what abstract artists are always telling us? But can they offer hope?" There is an aching beauty and sadness in Hank's play, especially when Pronk has a speech about missing fathers, and the children we all once were. We never get to see the reunion between Pronk and his son, but we do see a boy in the end. He is perhaps the ghost of Pronk's lost or dead son (plane crash?), or the ghost of Pronk himself when he was a boy. A very powerful five pages. In another corner of the loft was a bar where Guy Zimmerman staged his play *Pink*. Someone is always in danger in Guy's plays, but you don't necessarily want to warn them—you'd rather see how it plays out in the twists and turns of Guy's language. We are in a weird bar. A man whose girlfriend was last seen there questions the bartender: "Left my woman friend sitting right there on that barstool. She was deep in conversation with the barkeep. That barkeep was you." But the bartender avoids this interaction and instead offers his services politely: "What'll it be tonight sir?" What happened to the woman? The language suggests possibilities. Perhaps the man left her there on purpose, or made a deal with the bartender to keep her there. Or maybe she and the bartender entered into some sort of secret agreement. This is a fucked-up situation that excited me as an audience member! Juarez and other places of horror are mentioned. The woman has haunted the man's thoughts and he wakes up thinking of demons, as at last the woman Adele emerges, telling the men that she is pregnant. But by whom, or what? The three characters are connected by some dark thread that is being played out in this bar, perhaps forever. It truly was a magical evening as we moved around the loft for other plays, with occasional glimpses of the downtown skyline and moon. . .

I was taken to a concert at The Folly Bowl by a friend who thought it would make a good place for the kind of theater I was doing. I had no idea what to expect and was blown away by the generosity of these folks—performance curators and homeowners Susanna Dadd and James Griffith, who have been hosting annual concerts and dance performances at their home in Altadena for many years. I approached them after the concert and told them a little about myself, and then asked to see if they might be interested in hosting theater. They had never hosted plays at The Folly Bowl before, so we were the first! Audiences sit in their beautiful sloping yard, which is embedded with creeping vines, odd potted plants and stone benches—as if it has been excavated and you are picnicking on an archeological site (food and drink are encouraged at The Folly

Bowl!), all while looking down on an improvised stage. You are outside of Los Angeles and up in the hills in Altadena, and the rustic quality adds to a sense of the timelessness of theater, telling stories to each other outside, as human beings have done for eons. I produced a few summers of shows there, including plays by Wes Walker, Chris Kelley, and Michael Hacker. It is a profound treat to experience the titillation of a Wes Walker play, to hear the actors speak his mad and alluring words, to be taken on the dark, wild ride that is always present in his work. *Giant Hollow Tooth* brings together a woman and her architect son, who is trying to realize the dream of a demented "captain" (self-proclaimed or of what, we do not need to know): to build "the greatest shopping structure of porcelain... where you'll hear sobbing in the food court, the memory of a people drained... people will shop until they are nauseous." We hear about the plans in their early stages and then witness the charismatic nut of a captain gesturing a little too much with his sword, cutting the woman and himself repeatedly. We don't know where this world is, but there is a "desert beyond, where human hope cooks." Animals and people will have to be sacrificed for this "mall," which ends in eventual ruin, the emblem of a consumer culture possibly turning in on and eating itself. It reminded me of one of J. G. Ballard's (a favorite writer of mine) dystopian worlds, where man is gone (or in the process of disappearing) and nature has thrived in mysterious and possibly dangerous ways. In Chris Kelley's eerie two-person play *Those Who Get Close*, the woman calls her partner "a lost man waiting for someone in a dark place." We are transported to a barn where a man, Bill, has holed himself away, enduring repeated Black Widow bites in order to suffer, and get to some sort of spiritual truth: "I am soon beset by the legs and mandibles of countless fever bringing beasties all gang and pumping god knows how much horror into my veins. Hopped on black poison, one sees with many eyes." His wife Stacy (long-suffering, perhaps from being married to him, but also with her own demons) stands nearby with a glass of wine, calling him to dinner. This could be a typical day, yet Bill never comes to dinner, and nothing is resolved. They continue to live side by side with their pain, which good times aside, is a part of marriage. Bill must continue with his self-imposed exile and visions, and his wife knows that, but she still makes her feelings known, "I can hear what you're thinking, hear every word Bill and you're wrong. The truth of love is, if you're lucky, it destroys absolutely and you don't have to do it yourself." What has happened to these people? Stacy asks, "Who listens? You're alone, bleating at empty heaven for all the world like a thousand liars." Both are troubled by their missing son, but they can't do anything about it. Bill howls, and Stacy listens nearby. The play is full of beautiful language and a dark poetry. Even though the actors are standing on an empty stage, all of the scenery and effects are vividly painted for us with the language. Michael Hacker's play *All Around The World* takes us to an old Hollywood estate of mysterious history. Echo, a woman, has been hanging out there, but she doesn't know anything about the house. Elias encounters her, claiming to work for the unseen man (El Patron) who owns it. There is something wonderfully noirish in a contemporary way in Michael's play; Echo isn't your typical female in distress, but she is attractive, mysterious, and there is something exotic about her—she claims to have run away from the circus. There is a sadness about her, perhaps because she is nomadic, a woman with no home. As Elias measures the property and creeps around with a flashlight, we feel like we're there with him. The environs of the estate are themselves a character (I'm a huge believer in the offstage world), as is

Los Angeles. Elias says, "I drove in last night, I don't know a soul here. I can't understand what I'm seeing out there. It's not a city like other cities I've seen." Echo responds, "The valley is hard and bright, and the city is soft and dull. A person going from one to the other transforms." El Patron finally shows up, spouting off about his plans for the place, and the men leave Echo alone, as she was. The play reminded me of another one of my favorite places in L.A., Runyon Canyon, that has the ruins of Errol Flynn's mansion at its base. Michael was one of the first people I met when I was introduced to Padua, and I love talking to him about L.A. He is also a talented photographer, and his photographs show his love for the underbelly and the unusual of this city.

The other plays of my own that I have chosen for this anthology reflect sites and ideas that I was very excited to use. *Your Husband's Friend* was set in front of an open garage. Garages have always intrigued me, as they house things we can't quite get rid of but that are neglected, which is sad, like personal items you might find in a thrift store of a long dead owner. When a person is gone all that is left is their things. They can be replaced, but not the person. Garages are also dark and house recluse spiders. The actors stood in front of my open garage for the entire play about loss and divorce, while the audience crowded around. *Small Planet* was an experiment that I would love to do again. It required a small audience that would follow behind the actors as they took a stroll, something I very much enjoy doing, especially in the hills of Silver Lake and Echo Park, near my home. The play was written with the rhythm of being on a walk with no destination in mind. I wanted the subject matter to have that lilting feel of conversation coupled with walking. As the audience followed the actors and listened, dogs barked at us as we passed by, a bumblebee almost stung one of the actors, and a helicopter whirred overhead. My plan was to do this play several times with different audiences following different routes through the hills that I had mapped out.

This is the wonder of site-specific theater. You get these delightful, sometimes niggling interruptions that add layers of randomness and reality to the experience. In the controlled environment of a theater, you might not discover that you have a "garage" play inside you. I hope to be able to do more site-specific theater; I have a list of places: abandoned subway tunnels and meat lockers, among others. I can't always get permission to do them, but I when I do, it's magic for me, the actors, and I think the audience as well.

Last, I want to mention my relationship with Guy Zimmerman. He is one of my favorite L.A. writers. I squirm sometimes while hearing his characters speak the emotional darkness in their hearts, and I love that. We've laughed a lot and enjoyed hearing each other's work. He has been a strong force of support, and is incredibly smart. We've been "doing theater" off and on together for over twenty years now, which is amazing. This collaborative book was his idea.

Writing is ultimately a solitary task. But what's equally important is coming together to speak about ideas and hear each other's work. Finding a group of people whose writing you love, who force you to strive to be a better writer, isn't easy. I don't know if it's luck or Kismet that I found these people, but I am very grateful.

The Party

by Sharon Yablon

The Party was presented by Sharon's Farm in the lobby of the
Sunset Hotel, 2003, under the direction of the playwright, with the
following cast:

MARY	*Andy Stein*
ELISABETH	*Mary Greening*
MIRABELLE	*Dana Wieluns*
LES	*Gill Gayle*
LYDIA	*Kim Debus*
ELAINE	*Tina Preston*

Characters

MARY   *A head turner who is traumatized by her own beauty.*

ELISABETH   *A young woman. Dismissive of others, obsessed with her sister, MIRABELLE.*

MIRABELLE   *ELISABETH's younger sister, coy and unpredictable; she is just realizing the power of her sexuality.*

LES   *Roving eye, legend in his own mind, LYDIA's boyfriend.*

LYDIA   *Insecure and overly accessorized.*

ELAINE   *A middle-aged homeless lesbian. She lives among the environs of the house.*

Setting

The play takes place during a party at ELISABETH's and MIRABELLE's house, an estate in the hills of Los Angeles that's falling apart. A balmy, summer night in August.

(1950s music. ELISABETH and MIRABELLE on a stairwell. Both wear long dresses and gloves. They slow dance together. MARY enters, carrying a plastic cup. She is dressed a little slutty.)

Mary	Hello?
Elisabeth	Oh god. Somebody's here already.
Mirabelle	Escort me downstairs!

(They slowly descend the stairs to the lobby.)

I saw a coyote running along our street today. Boys were chasing it and screaming. That's when I saw the retarded girl, Alba. Her brother had left her alone. She sat in the carport of her parents' house, one finger in her vagina. The boys came back then. Blood on their faces...

Elisabeth	Tell me more.
Mirabelle	There's nothing more to tell.

(They walk past MARY.)

Elisabeth	You think you're going to meet somebody tonight, isn't that true?
Mirabelle	Yes, I've tired of you.
Elisabeth	Don't count on it.

(They survey the audience, their potential party guests.)

Elisabeth	There's Larry. He's into porn.

Mirabelle	*(Smiling.)* Yeah.
Elisabeth	He's ignoring Mary. Just look at her over there.

(MARY *reluctantly approaches them.*)

Mary	Hi.
Mirabelle	*(Phony.)* Hi!
Elisabeth	This is my sister, Mirabelle.
Mary	Your sister? I thought you were. Well.
Elisabeth	What? Speak up!
Mirabelle	Yes, speak up!
Mary	Lesbians.

(ELISABETH and MIRABELLE both laugh.)

Elisabeth	Of course not! We're sisters.
Mirabelle	*(Suddenly stares at MARY.)* You're pretty.
Mary	I know, but it doesn't make me happy. You're both pretty too, but your eyes are too small for your faces. I'm sorry, I don't really know what to say to people at parties.
Elisabeth	It's awkward. Hiding what you feel all the time, isn't it Mary?
Mirabelle	Sometimes we say things we don't want to. Our panties become sticky. The fun begins. We like parties.
Elisabeth	*(Suddenly points.)* Look at her! With the shoulder pads! Who is she?!
Mirabelle	I spotted her today, walking with a man in town. She was looking at him but he didn't notice her. It was sad. I went up to her and whispered in her ear, we're having a party tonight. But don't bring him. He doesn't love you.

Mary	(*Looking around.*) Where's Larry?
Elisabeth	It seems he brought you to this party and then left you!
Mary	He blindfolds me. We did this all day yesterday. His hands are cold, and the blindfold smelled of animal husbandry. But I'm so lonely, even though I'm pretty.
Mirabelle	How did that make you feel?
Mary	Sad. A little turned on. He propped me against the wall. I tried to clutch at it, even though there was nothing to clutch. Men like that, I think.

(*ELISABETH examines MARY's fingernails.*)

Elisabeth	It's paint alright.
Mary	This is a lovely house.
Elisabeth	And now it's ours! Aren't inheritances fun?!
Mary	They're actually very sad occasions.
Mirabelle	Maybe people will wander around and start to screw in all the rooms!

(*ELAINE crosses behind the women, carrying a big plate of food. She is barefoot and unkempt. Halfway through she looks at the women and scowls.*)

Mirabelle	My room is locked.
Elisabeth	So is mine.
Mirabelle	Because it's the same room.
Mary	You share a room?
Elisabeth	Yes.

Mary	Isn't that strange?
Elisabeth	Why?
Mary	Two adult sisters together in the same room?
Elisabeth	We were home schooled. We didn't get the chance to develop proper social skills.
Mirabelle	We fall asleep every night in each other's arms.
Elisabeth	Telling terrible stories.
Mirabelle	Here's one! Today I was in a 7-11.
Elisabeth	That's terrible, say no more!
Mirabelle	A scrawny Chinese man came in and took note of me. He was much too old for me, and I followed him.
Elisabeth	What do you mean?!
Mirabelle	(*Avoiding ELISABETH, to MARY.*) Are your parents still alive?
Elisabeth	Yes, are they?
Mary	No.
Elisabeth	What happened?
Mirabelle	Did a tragedy befall your family?
Mary	Yes, that's exactly what happened. But you were at the funerals.
Elisabeth	How sad that we could have forgotten.
Mirabelle	You've got a piece of hair in your mouth.

(*MIRABELLE slides her finger along MARY's lips, they have a "moment."*)

Mary	The tragedy caused me to become promiscuous. I guess you could call me a sex addict. What happened with the Chinese man you followed?

Mirabelle	He walked into a little house with plaster of Paris gnomes. I knocked on the door. When he answered he seemed nervous. We sat at a large wood table, and spread out over it were those mailers of missing people. What are you doing with those? I asked. Do you want some tea? Yes, but what are you doing with those?
Mary	When I showered this morning, there was a little blood.
Mirabelle	Blood?
Mary	From my bottom.
Mirabelle	(*Excited.*) Oh! Tell us about it, on the verandah!

(*The sisters turn slightly.*)

Elisabeth	People talk about us.
Mirabelle	They throw rocks through the windows.
Elisabeth	There's one over there. We used it to keep the door to our bedroom shut. Sometimes Father. In our bedroom. Mary. (*Hides her face in her hands.*)
Mirabelle	Mary. (*Hides her face in her hands.*)
Mary	I think it's very inconsiderate of Larry to neglect me like this.
Elisabeth	Well then, leave him!
Mary	Yes. But then you break up, and you run into him somewhere and think. Remember? You were everything once, and now you're nothing. It's too painful.
Mirabelle	Turn around then. Let's see your body!

(*MARY turns around slowly.*)

Mary	My last boyfriend made me eat in private. But it always ends, and then I'm here. Alone, at parties.
Mirabelle	Aren't you a drunk?
Elisabeth	We've heard stories about you, wandering in homes with panties twirled around your fingers and frosty lipstick.
Mary	I get depressed. I need to be around people.
Mirabelle	If we're all very quiet, Elaine will come out of the shrubs to look in the window. She wants in, with her dirty thoughts!
Mary	Who's Elaine?
Mirabelle	Somebody I met in a bar.

(*Angry at* MIRABELLE, ELISABETH *flirts with* MARY *and touches her hair.*)

Elisabeth	It's all real?
Mary	Yes.

(ELISABETH *pulls* MARY*'s hair a little.*)

Mary	Ouch! I'm going to find Larry.

(*She walks away.* MIRABELLE *follows her and* ELISABETH *follows* MIRABELLE.)

Mirabelle	Hurry, before you dry up like a gooseberry!

(LES *and* LYDIA *enter. They are in the midst of a conversation.* LYDIA *carries a cup and gazes at him.*)

Les	The people on the island turned on each other then. Disemboweled one another! Under the bright moon.
Lydia	But why did it happen?
Les	Well, it's anthropological.

(*Impressed, LYDIA serves LES his drink.*)

Les	Hey, it's empty!

(*ELISABETH and MIRABELLE turn into each other.*)

Mirabelle	What's the worst thing about you?
Elisabeth	I don't miss people when they leave. And you?
Mirabelle	I don't want anyone to be happy.

(*They giggle. LES sees MARY and approaches her. LYDIA follows LES. LES can't take his eyes off MARY.*)

Les	That's a very pretty dress.
Mary	Thank you, but I'll probably return it. I don't deserve nice things. I have too much anal sex.
Les	Oh boy!
Mary	Not just with my boyfriend, but with all his friends, and his cousins, and all their friends. I say I don't know what I'm doing, but I do.
Lydia	Hello, I'm Lydia. Les's live-in girlfriend.
Les	(*Sighs.*) Yes, I live with a woman. Her name is Lydia. There was a time when I worshipped her. She flat out told me, I will never love you Les, for several reasons. But now the tables have turned, haven't they Lydia?

Lydia	(*Looks down.*) Yes.
Les	What have the tables done?
Lydia	They've turned.

(*ELAINE enters and grabs a guest's purse. She exits.*)

Les	That's right! I ignored her. Women love that. Now, we live together. She farts in bed and eats string cheese. The worst of it is, she kisses like a lost, baby fish. A small open mouth that's fearful, looking for grubs. (*Mimics a bad kisser.*) She doesn't understand eroticism; I try to instruct her. Lydia, this is erotic. No Lydia, that is not erotic when you do that.
Lydia	What was I doing?
Les	Little fingers like baby spiders, running along my back. She loves me... (*Looks off, afraid.*)
Lydia	Do you want some fruit? Some cold shellfish? I could feed you. No? What do you want?!
Les	(*Ignores her.*) Hey, are you two lesbians?
Lydia	Why did you pursue me and then stop liking me when you got me?
Les	The string cheese, the Middle Eastern music, those stupid floppy velvet hats, the unemployment, the dead cats.
Lydia	It's true, I have cats. And they die. I don't know what it is I'm doing wrong.
Les	You can't keep anything alive is what it is.
Elisabeth	(*To LYDIA.*) That's the worst thing about you, then!
Mirabelle	What happens to the cats?
Lydia	The kittens get stepped on because they match our carpet.

(*MIRABELLE smiles.*)

Lydia   Les. . .?

Les   What?! (*Softens.*) Well get us some more of those little weenies or something. It'll be okay.

(*He kisses her reluctantly.*)

Mirabelle   He's repulsive.

Lydia   Les used to repulse me, too. The sight of him, that squat body. His disdain for people. "What are you doing," my girlfriends asked when I moved in with him. At our housewarming party he went right up to my friend Becca and told her that her nipples were like thimbles. Remember that, Les? Nipples like thimbles?

Les   Nope.

Lydia   All those paintings of dolphins he has around our house.

Les   *My* house, and they're smart, fool.

Lydia   I can destroy him, I thought. It'll be fun and then I can leave. But something happened. I crossed over. Into love.

Elisabeth   You must try to connect with those initial feelings of repulsion.

Les   I'm great in bed!

Lydia   He's not. But I love him.

Elisabeth   Stop that talk about love or you'll have to leave!

Mirabelle   We hate couples!

Lydia   I touch myself constantly when Les leaves the room.

Les   What?! (*A mood comes over him.*) Staring out at nothing, in a room. That is what frightens me most about aging.

Mary	What about your looks?
Elisabeth	They begin to fade in your thirties. Like the color draining out of a person's face who's just heard terrible news.
Les	I don't think I have to worry about all that. I was never handsome. And now suddenly this woman is in love with me! This has never happened to me before. I mean look at her. She's no dog. She has intellectual interests. She draws. She makes homemade jerked chicken. Where did you learn to do that?
Lydia	I told you, Ravi.
Les	Yeah, I hate that guy.
Lydia	He was a lover of mine. He's Indian, and he had nipples the color of eggplant. And guess what else?
Mirabelle	Oh!

(*ELISABETH glares at MIRABELLE.*)

Les	She threw me a surprise party. It was nice but I had nothing to say to her. How did I get to be so cruel?
Mirabelle	Everyone's capable of cruelty.
Lydia	(*Trying to get a reaction out of LES.*) Well, I've found a great apartment.

(*LES looks surprised. ELAINE looks at them through the window from outside.*)

Lydia	It comes furnished. Two transvestites live below me, and they are the kindest people. While their new sex organs are forming, I said I would help to distract them.

Les	Those are transsexuals, you idiot! Wait, I do love you!
Lydia	The transvestites quit their jobs and sit around all day renting movies and playing Yahtzee. Um.
Elisabeth	Speak up, wench!
Lydia	Who is that woman lurking outside?
Elisabeth	That's Elaine. She's in love with us both. She's a lesbian, and we can't have her around.
Mirabelle	She wanted to be in a relationship with me, but I said that I wasn't ready for a commitment.
Mary	My relationships with men never go anywhere. I don't use a condom, so they'll be back. In my life, there is little joy.
Les	Mine neither.

(*LES and MARY smile at each other. LYDIA is hurt.*)

Les	Did you really have anal sex with all those men?
Mary	Possibly.
Les	Do you like it?
Mary	Sort of.

(*LES and MARY walk away together. ELISABETH holds out her arm and MIRABELLE links hers with it.*)

| Elisabeth | (*To LYDIA.*) Nobody gets love from the one they want. Get a hold of yourself! |
| Mirabelle | You can always go back to diddling your clitty! |

(*They exit. ELAINE's voice is heard from somewhere.*)

| Elaine | Hey! You! |

(*LYDIA is still dejected about LES.*)

Elaine   When was the last time you had your pussy licked?

(*Intrigued, LYDIA looks around.*)

Elaine   I mean, *really* licked?

(*LYDIA meanders toward the voice. ELAINE pops out. Her clothes are falling apart and there is dirt on her face.*)

Lydia   Am I ugly?

Elaine   There's nothing worse than an ugly woman.

Lydia   What will happen to us?

Elaine   We'll still be fucked a lot.

Lydia   Who will fuck us?

Elaine   Everyone! Then we'll be cast out, and we'll find a new world. A world with no money. Won't that be fun?

Lydia   Yes.

(*ELAINE scratches her head and a bird's nest falls out.*)

Elaine   What's your favorite position?

Lydia   Um, how long have you been outside like this?

Elaine   I'm not sure... I had to get away from my apartment too. I have this friend, Dave. He's a theater director, and one night, just for the heck of it, I went down on him with an energy I had not known before. After that Dave wouldn't go away. He phoned. He wrote poems. Things like "There's nothing more lonely than a cocaine binge by yourself, a train whistle, and being without you." We screwed a lot in motels. Then I said, there will be no more of this, Dave. But why? He pleaded. I don't need a reason, you idiot! I told him. Then one day he came over. He had been neglecting himself, and there was a stench. He said to me, no one will love you like this again.

Lydia	Was he right?
Elaine	Yes. Where did you grow up?
Lydia	Here. Where did you grow up?
Elaine	In Simi Valley. Look at all the stars!

(LYDIA *looks up and* ELAINE *pinches her butt.*)

Lydia   Ouch.

Elisabeth and Mirabelle

(*From offstage.*) Hey bitches! (*They giggle.*)

Lydia	Those girls are so mean.
Elaine	Tell me about losing your virginity!
Lydia	It hurt. But a week before, my boyfriend put his fist up there, so.
Elaine	That's rad! Wanna hear about me?
Lydia	Okay.
Elaine	It was with my neighbor Gavin. He was slow. You know?
Lydia	Retarded?
Elaine	Yeah, so I took advantage of him! And he loved it! He was so hard, all the time.
Lydia	Are women less cruel to each other?
Elaine	Nothing lasts. Want to see my pussy?
Lydia	Do I have to?

Elaine	Yes, absolutely!

(ELAINE *tries to get herself into the best "viewing" position.*)

Elaine	Ow! Fuck!
Lydia	Are you okay?
Elaine	Fuckin' yoga.
Lydia	Do you think you could love me?
Elaine	Love goes away. Now come down here and say hello.
Lydia	(*Slowly kneels down.*) But I don't know what to do.
Elaine	It's like riding a bike.
Lydia	Will you call me?
Elaine	No.
Lydia	Nobody stays with me.
Elaine	Me neither. But think I care? Nope!

(MIRABELLE *enters.* LIGHTS *change. Outdoor sounds.*)

Mirabelle	My father told me that he never should have gotten married. And could I forgive him? (*Wanders further out.*) You can hear the coyotes, after a kill. They come onto our property sometimes. Pupils glowing. Our eyes meet. Neither of us knows how we got here. (*Moves around the stage area.*) There's a series of stilt houses over there. The architect went insane. Strange vegetation. Snakes and skulls. Ghosts of Indians and wild chickens. From up here you can get a sense of how big Los Angeles is. How vast. Someone came up with a

grid. Drew lines into the dirt. Back when people didn't leave the house without a hat. When the air was pure, and the Black Dahlia was still alive. She hadn't even come here yet. She was just a girl. A beautiful stranger. Now, everyone knows who she is. (*MIRABELLE looks off. Music. Slow fade as she wanders into the hills.*)

The End

The Virtue of Hospitality

by Bernard Goldberg

The Virtue of Hospitality *was presented by Sharon's Farm around the yard and pool at her parents' house in Beverly Hills, 2003. It was directed by the playwright with the following cast:*

AVI	*Rick Dean*
SARAH LEE	*Mary Greening*
WAITER	*Gregory Littman*
WAITRESS	*Susanna Schulten*

Avi	Have you been to the Dead Sea, where your cares slip away in an oily film, like Oil of Olay, that lubricates your body so you feel young? Or like baby oil and you're cared for, and someone watches over you?
Sarah Lee	It's hot there, isn't it?
Avi	Hundred and three in the summer. But the air is filled with bromides. Natural tranquilizers. It feels rather pleasant.
	I was there once with my nephew. He and his wife, they had some trouble with their daughters. I don't know, I don't remember. I try not to get involved.
	They were told to leave town. Get out, they were told, and don't look back.
	What brings you here?
Sarah Lee	I like to swim. How about you?
Avi	I like to swim. I try not to.
	We do well to contain certain impulses but not at the expense of the world's joy.
Sarah Lee	That is my problem. That is my problem in a nutshell.
Avi	I feel we understand each other, you and I. Your experience leaves you in search of the authentic. The authentic stands against a backdrop of stagnation. Stagnation is a term used often for water. People too can stagnate. Like water. Like people stuck in little pools, their fingers forming ripples on the surface of the sludge.

Sarah Lee	Where there is water, we might immerse ourselves in it. Water that means something, ritual water, something more than recreation. Maybe not. That means a great deal.
Avi	You said you had a problem.
Sarah Lee	No.
Avi	You said you had a problem and I touched on it.
Sarah Lee	Are you sure?
Avi	Yes. Now we're getting somewhere.
Sarah Lee	In my bed sometimes, I lean back against the pillow, my arms around my knees, and I look at what I've done, I see it as it happens, over and over again, and each time I see it there's a second when I understand that what I'm doing is wrong, and I can stop it. If I were thinking clearly, or clearly enough, I could take in this passing awareness that what I'm in the process of doing is wrong. I can see for an instant that what I'm doing should be stopped, and yet I don't stop.
Avi	I can tell you about my nephew now. He stayed with me, learning from my habits, watching me as I entered the world and improved it. I did that, improve the world. I told myself maybe I'm not good enough to do that. Maybe I'm not a good enough person to improve the world. But I am. I'm someone, as you are, who can go to a person and help him. You can look at a person, figure out what she needs.
Sarah Lee	What's your nephew's name?
Avi	Why does that matter? This is a story. I'm telling you a story. I'm creating a world that may be of benefit. Although specific, it has a general message. I don't know.

I don't mean to be hostile. My nephew admired me, and I did my best to teach him. I did my best to help him. When he imperiled my name by imposing on my neighbors, I told him to leave. Left or right, I told him, north or south. Pick one, and be on your way.

Sarah Lee   Your story illustrates the importance of family, but more so the difficulties. The challenges of helping while at the same time maintaining borders.

Avi   I don't know what that means. My nephew stepped on my help. My respect for him left, though not my love. I can love without respect, but I cannot live without love, if that makes any sense.

Sarah Lee   Once again, what began as a conversation with the potential to be enlightening has ended as an ordinary chat.

(*WAITER enters.*)

Waiter   Hello!

Here are your complimentary drinks.

I'll give you a few moments to enjoy your margaritas.

(*Pause.*)

These lushy green areas, these retreaty resorts.

People sunbathe, they drink. They float sometimes, dead center, in the middle of a pool.

(*Pause.*)

I'm serving you now. I'm bringing you drinks. I'm relieving you of the burden to engage in conversation. I'm leaving you with something to talk about when I'm gone. You may say of me, He's rude. He's late. He's confused. I don't mind at all. I'm happy to be here.

(*Pause.*)

I moved to this city by the sea to be selfless. It wasn't at all for myself.

My neighbors were friendly in an unctuous sort of way. We had neighborhood meetings, little league games, rugby matches, Superbowl parties, trips to Las Vegas, rites of spring fests, gossip get-togethers, and lottery rituals.

I wanted to help people. I would try to improve the world. My plan was to teach by example and by lecture.

But just in case . . .

I'll be back with more salt for your margaritas.

(*Waiter exits.*)

Sarah Lee   You're afraid of me, aren't you?
Avi   How did you know?

44

Sarah Lee	I can feel these things. Whenever I'm near water, my skin becomes translucent. There's a light inside my bones. You might say bones are links, that they connect one thing with another. I wouldn't say that, even though it's true.
	I've floated in the Dead Sea.
Avi	You didn't tell me that.
Sarah Lee	I stepped out gingerly on the sharp, hot rocks, out into the middle of the roped off area, and lay on my back and floated around, paddling myself around as I looked up at the hills.
Avi	In one direction, the hills of Jordan. In the other, the Judean hills.
Sarah Lee	I've been there, yes.
	I heard about your nephew.
	His wife turned to salt.
Avi	It's the Dead Sea. It does that to people.
Sarah Lee	Sometimes, yes. But now it tends to heal. From all over the world, people come to take the waters. I am going, they say, to the spa to take the waters.
Avi	We don't exactly know what turned her to salt.
	I have my thoughts, of course.
	The people in my nephew's city hated strangers and would rob them of their money. When the victim

complained, the courts fined him. After inviting a stranger into his home, the resident attacked him and robbed him and demanded that he sleep. Then he'd tear off the stranger's legs to make him fit the bed.

My nephew learned kindness from me, the virtue of hospitality. It may not matter to you because the value of a good host has been forgotten over time, but before everyone became a stranger, a host could bring comfort to your journey.

Sarah Lee   There must be an art to it. Giving just what the person needs, no more, no less. Remaining unobtrusive. Making your guest feel welcome without the slightest air of imposition or resentment.

Avi   Every night, my nephew wandered the streets looking for strangers he could help. He'd bring them home, send for food, and fill their jars with water. In the morning, he'd give them washcloths and invite them to use the bath.

The neighbors learned that my nephew had just invited two guests into his home, and the entire city crowded in front of his door and demanded the strangers be given to them. I'm happy to say my nephew had some principles and refused to turn them over. But what I'll probably never understand is that he offered his daughters instead.

Sarah Lee   Maybe in his own way, he was trying to be a good host.

Avi   Maybe he misunderstood my message.

(*WAITRESS enters.*)

Waitress   My husband asked me to check on you, to see if there's anything you might want.

He asked me to watch you, to see what people look like when they're enjoying themselves.

My husband's a wonderful waiter, don't you think? When he runs out of something, he sends me to the neighbors to get it. Or he sends me out here to ask the guests how they are.

How are you? Is everything okay? Is there anything you need? If there is, I'll run over to the neighbors.

The neighbors and I get along. We share stories. We complain. I try not to say too much because anyone who shows kindness, particularly toward strangers, is killed. I try not to say too much.

My husband and our daughters have an unnatural attraction for each other. The neighbors say he sublimates his urges by walking late at night.

(*Pause.*)

Have you swum in our water? Some people say swam. My daughters say that. Have you swam in our waters?

But it's swum.

I have swum. You have swum. He have swum. She have swum.

(*Pause.*)

You're probably thinking my husband is more gracious than me.

(*Pause.*)

I'll be back in a moment with your food.

(*WAITRESS exits.*)

Sarah Lee	You can't live in a city like that without becoming infected.
Avi	Everyone was wealthy. Gold grew next to vegetables, and a penny multiplied to three. The people became insatiable. They could never get enough money, pleasure, or pain. Even earthquakes were not enough to warn them. Maybe my nephew learned as much from them as he did from me.
Sarah Lee	Maybe he offered his daughters to the crowd because he knew the crowd would reject them.
Avi	I don't see how that would have helped.
Sarah Lee	Maybe it gave him time.
Avi	Until the crowd went blind.

Sarah Lee	Still, he should have been turned to salt. Instead of his wife.
Avi	I should have taught him to die for his family instead of sacrificing them for himself.
Sarah Lee	The Dead Sea's filled with salt. He would have blended in, become a sculpture on the side of a hill.
	Instead of his wife, who wasn't even mentioned until the end of the story.
Avi	His wife told her neighbors about the guests when she went to borrow salt from them.
Sarah Lee	I didn't know that.
Avi	Along the surface of the water is a border, and this border has a life, as does everything. And the border separates the world of water from the world of air, and at the edges of the water is a border, and this border has a life, as does everything.
	The truth about borders is not that they separate, though they do. It's that they link things, one to another. You, for example, think you're separate from me, and this air between us is a border. But maybe that's not true.
Sarah Lee	Maybe it isn't. I go down to the water sometimes, any water. At the ocean, the waves are vertical, forming hills against the sky, unstable hills that break and crumble. In rivers, waters stream along the banks, struggling with the land that contains them. Then I go to pools, pools of swimming, blue and pure with floors of pebbled cement.

In water you can dream of a future. You can remember who you are. You can crystallize and clarify yourself into a fluid body of water linking you and all the others, all of you together in a mindless, selfless sea. I think that may be true.

The End

Shy

by April Rouveyrol

Shy *was presented by Sharon's Farm, Wattles Park, 2004, under the direction of the playwright, with the following cast:*

MISTY *Jenny Eakes*
RAY *Maury Sterling*

(A quiet moment in the middle of the park by a dried up waterfall. We're really in a girl's bedroom indoors. MISTY is huddled in front of the would-be waterfall as if she's sitting on a bed—she's fantasizing she's in a park. She is in her twenties but has the mannerisms of a teenage girl. She is beautiful, whip-smart, open heart, frightened mind. She talks fast. Manic. As she speaks the figure of a MAN starts moving down the hill weaving in and out of the foliage/trees. He makes his way down to the ridge above MISTY and regards her through her speech. She senses him and looks around trying to find him throughout her speech.)

Misty   Okay, I have my hat, sunglasses, my inner scarf, my outer scarf. I always get a little tense before my outing. My mother makes me—forces me to go *outside* for lunch once a month. See the scratch marks on the walls from this experience? I told her that I will not go to Beverly Hills, I will not go to Sunset Plaza—I will not go anywhere on the west side specifically north of the 10 freeway or perpendicular to the 5. I—me—I get to choose the place. It was Clifton's Cafeteria in Glendora. However the SOB tie flung over the shoulder management ball-lickers closed the Clifton's Cafeteria one year and a half ago. With my special place annihilated I had to find another favorite little haunt. After spurning numerous suggestions of my mothers' I went south as that's the thing to do when lost—head south. I found a cafeteria in a retirement home that I liked.

(RAY *unzips his pants and faces a tree. One leg up on a* *mound. He looks at her over his shoulder until he's* *done.* MISTY *pretends not to notice. She keeps talking.* RAY *does tai chi.*)

Misty   The Great Day Retirement Villa in Fontana. They serve lunch daily from 11:30 A.M. to 1:30 P.M. and welcome visitors. They do a really good turkey meatloaf. I bundle up in my outfit and I leave my lamp—my bedside lamp—*on*—A light burns for me. Are you listening?

Ray   Re—pulse mon—key. I'm listening with my body. I'm absorbing what you're saying and sending it back to you.

Misty   The outdoors is just not for everyone. See. Books are my friends, you know? The Brönte sisters, Turgenev, Faulkner, a little Nieztsche—Webster—that's a book— he's a friend. Webster says my condition is a fear of open spaces or situations where escape might be difficult. Seeeee—?

Ray   Open spaces—open to the sky and all the angels—where you might meet people. Someone.

(RAY *moves around on his cliff looking for another spot* *to position himself. He finds one. Faces another tree,* *unzips his pants and stretches his back.* RAY *looks over* *at* MISTY. RAY *is both creepy and sexy. She notices but* *tries not to.*)

Ray   How's this angle? Good? Better? Not the same?

(*She ignores him.*)

Misty   Okay. I have my hat—Sunglasses—My inner scarf—My outer scarf—

(R*AY walks over to the edge of the cliff, kneels and talks to her gently.*)

Ray   I forgot. What's your name?

Misty   Misty. It's Misty. A tragic name. My mother was unstable at the time. I think. You ever notice names like Misty—Summer—Crystal are always these girls on the evening news who are kidnapped and their bodies found near Barstow or they need this eleventh hour operation to transplant their kidney. You notice that?

Ray   Now Misty, I have not always lived in squalor. Perhaps that's what you think of me? Perhaps that's where you place me? In a box on the street. Fleabag hotel. Studio apartment in El Monte? One light bulb swinging. Squalor to you is romantic. Squalor to you is idealistic. Isn't that right? Isn't that a statement about my politics and the kind of car I drive. Am I safe? A man who is safe? Do you think I'd hurt you? You look really pale.

(M*ISTY is silent.*)

So you remember the park?

Misty   The park. Refresh my memory.

(*RAY walks towards her and slowly slips off one of her scarfs from around her neck.*)

Ray	That guy you met.
Misty	Out there. In the park.
Ray	Remember him?
Misty	Yeah. That guy. So?
Ray	You're Misty... and what was his name?

(*She doesn't answer.*)

	Did he scare you? Did he touch you? Did his presence offend you? Or did he give you goose bumps all over—?
Misty	Ray. Like a sting ray. He was Argentinian. He told me when there's lightning that God is taking a picture of him. Nice ego.
Ray	So you talked to him? Ray.
Misty	Talked—? No.
Ray	Did you think about him?
Misty	Yeah. That maybe he went straight from that tree in the park to doing something horrible.
Ray	Horrible? Like what? What would Ray do?
Misty	I don't know. Maybe he left the park, robbed a Bank of America, raped a teller, fed a hamburger to a cow, went to prison and then he and I became pen pals and sent letters about the wonders of our common experiences of confinement and lack of sun.
Ray	Maybe he went straight from that tree in the park to Ibiza where he found a lover, loved her, had a baby and is living quite happily right now.

Misty	That's funny.
Ray	Well he never did meet you, right? You met or you didn't meet?
Misty	I don't know I don't know.
Ray	Shouldn't you be graduating high school or applying to college or something?
Misty	Should be. Could be.
Ray	(*Creepy.*) Or doing something useful like climbing a tree naked?
Misty	You're some kind of pedophile right?
Ray	You're not a child. I'm not a pedophile.
Misty	You're flirting? Good job. I'm not well.
Ray	So the last time you were outside. How long ago? Four or five years?

(*MISTY regards him with suspicion and is quiet.*)

Those are critical years to be locked in a room.
Adolescence came and went and you weren't there. I
always wondered what bright people did when cut off.

Misty	Not cut off. Sheltered. With roof. (*MISTY clings to her bed sheet and wraps it around her torso.*)
Ray	Nice room.
Misty	It's a treasure trove.
Ray	You look really pale.
Misty	I'm so lacking in color and hue and contrast it makes me exotic. I am exotically pale. I am an albino queen living on my very own room island. Regard the indigenous vegetation on room island—one begonia.

Ray	Too much concrete.

(RAY is not listening and does some kind of suggestive hip or body stretch during the following.)

Misty	What does that mean? You're saying because I was raised in a conventional urban environment with buzzing sounds and little inanimate objects that you look at and pick up and talk to and watch and watch you because I've had very little exposure to goats and rivers and jumping on rocks, because I access the world through my iPad—and I think you're making an assumption. Your condescending crap comments about your disdain for mood stabilizers and how sleep is just a coping mechanism for misery. Pant. Pant.
Ray	The walls are fucking with your cabeza. (*He taps her head.*)
Misty	If you're about to burgle or rape me I really don't recommend it. I'm not well.
Ray	(*Laughs.*) Burgle you? Just stay... and I'll tell you about a girl I knew in Brazil. (*RAY gently removes her other scarf.*)
Misty	I am just un. As in uninterested. Unengaged. Unthetic. Whatever. And don't want to hear about your Brazilian girlfriend.
Ray	Her name was Lucilia Juvenilia. She taught me Portuguese and the sex was hot and we danced samba— you would like it. (*RAY moves seductively.*) What I remember about her is that she was deeply sad. She told me this story when we met how her baby died and she was mourning him and she later told me she made it up

	just so she wouldn't have to explain her unhappiness. That's just the way she was. It rained a lot and she would drinkraindropsfromundermyfingernailsanditwaserotic—
Misty	I see. I'm thinking. I'm trying to figure out this gem of a tale. No theme of fear or overcoming adversity and this is supposed to help me how?
Ray	You didn't like it? You afraid you'll wake up with me rolled in your sheets? Cause I'd like to spend a little time with you in your bedroom. I'd like to set the alarm for thirty minutes and do some things. But it's not what you're thinking.
Misty	Fear is a survival mechanism.
Ray	So maybe this guy in the park holding his dick is going to ruin you. Keep you in suspense every remaining day of your pitiful life. Maybe he's going to move to Nepal to stare at the turquoise sky or maybe he's going to fuck your best friend and steal all your money. But I tell you something, and you want to hear this, look at me not the begonia—are you listening?

(*MISTY stares at him.*)

You're not going to meet someone who electrifies
every cell in your body and turns you from stone to
liquid from a stranger to a lover. You're not going to
experience crossing the Atlantic and see a moon rainbow
for the first time. A tongue you barely know finding its
way down your neck. The possibilities flying by waiting
for you...

Misty	I have my sunglasses. My hat. My inner scarf. My... and I just want you to stop talking to me okay? Just leave me alone. I know what's not going to happen to me today. Okay? I know I'm not going to die in a plane crash. I know I'm not going to get hit by a car. I know I'm not going to contract an STD. Those are the simple dimple daddy long leg ones.
Ray	You're not going to have someone like me say something nice to you.
Misty	Like what would you say nice to me?
Ray	(RAY *thinks about it. Does some more tai chi—then—*) Just the thought of you warms my heart.

(*She likes that but it scares her.*)

Misty	Fear is a survival mechanism.
Ray	I know. You told me. Fear can make people do some very twisted things. Now I wonder what happened to Ray and Misty at the park. Do you think he did something bad to her or—maybe—she did something bad to him. Hmmm?

(*RAY begins to re-dress MISTY with her gear. Her hat. Her scarves. He plays with a scarf seductively around her neck. Then threatens her with it. Then releases it and lets it fall gently on her chest.*)

Ray	Well then, maybe you saw him out there pissing on a tree and it just made you... *shy.*

(RAY puts her sunglasses on her face and walks back up toward the ridge. She watches him. He walks over to the tree in his original position unzips his pants, props one leg up on a mound and turns his back to her. MISTY pulls her sunglasses off and looks at him.)

The End

The Asia Campaign

by Hank Bunker

The Asia Campaign *was presented by Sharon's Farm and Padua Playwrights, Bedlam Warehouse, 2006. It was directed by the playwright with the following cast:*

GREEVER   *Trace Turville Konerko*
PRONK   *George Gerdes*
BOY   *Edward Felix*

Setting

Conference room. Modular couch angled on two walls. Painting on one wall. Open window on other wall. A woman, GREEVER, sits in business attire with a laptop, back of head to open window. A man, PRONK, well-dressed, leans deeply against the cushions on couch, back of head to painting.

Greever	What are you thinking about, Mr. Pronk? Are you wondering if we haven't all embraced the online culture with just a bit too much fervor?
Pronk	I'm thinking about my son.
Greever	Let me start again. The words come but sometimes feel unconnected. The trick is to get behind the word before you push it out. To define it before it defines you. Reality is what you make it, Mr. Pronk. So I ask again, this time with confidence, is your son a freshman in high school?
Pronk	He is.
Greever	I thought so. I am paid to see around corners, and it's nice, let me tell you, to get paid for what one does naturally.
Pronk	He arrives tonight from the Philippines.
Greever	What's his flight number? I'll look him up. (*Pause.*) But he's en route, is he not, at this moment, above our heads? I'm struggling. I can feel it. I want to communicate. We're in the communication business. Still, it's as though with each word I get farther from the center. (*Slight pause.*) I find it helpful to talk these things out.

(PRONK *stands, regards painting on wall.*)

Pronk	This picture has never appeared to me the same way twice.
Greever	I want to reply. I have one ready. It's just that I find myself rather suddenly and unexpectedly behind the reality curve.

Pronk	What does this picture mean? Can you tell me?
Greever	I'll say this. Often I feel I'm one of these paintings myself, clotted over for centuries, while beneath, a Caravaggio suffocates.
Pronk	I can't understand it.
Greever	I'm sure it means that we're all lost in a godless void. Isn't that what abstract artists are always telling us? But can they offer hope? That's my question. Anybody can sip espresso and pretend it's 1952. The Cold War is over. The Nuclear Age is over. We've digested the horror. Move on! We *have* moved on. Some would say to bleaker horizons. But that's too easy. Giving up is easy. What's hard? Resisting—the impulse to be comfortable. That's what's hard. And to do that we need hope. Just a minute, I'm getting an Instant Message. It's from the IT department. Apparently, the whole phone system is down. Our conference call may be delayed. Well, they'd better hurry up because it's a ten-hour difference over there.
Pronk	What do you hope for?
Greever	A little bandwidth would be nice. Ever been to a hotel in Bulgaria? But seriously, what did you just say?
Pronk	I asked what you hope.
Greever	I hope your son makes it down safely. (*Pause.*) I'm not clairvoyant. I'm not trying to *say* anything. It's just sometimes I do manage to get behind the word before I cough it out. Let's change the subject. When was the last time you saw your son?
Pronk	Six years ago.

Greever	Since he was very young? My. You'll have a lot to talk about. It occurs to me that I have not changed the subject at all.
Pronk	I'm nervous.
Greever	About meeting your son?
Pronk	What does one talk about with a young person?
Greever	Does he have a Twitter account? Has he uploaded content onto YouTube? It's all about content at the moment, Mr. Pronk. Uploadable, downloadable, but particularly uploadable.
Pronk	Do you have children?
Greever	Me? No. No. None. One. Once. You know what it is? I figured it out. Tom is drunk after lunch and it's just past lunch over there. So here we sit, cooling our jets. Boy, these computers get hot on your knees.

(*She stands. Pause.*)

Pronk	What happened to your child?
Greever	Would you be interested in buying an anti-gravity chair, Mr. Pronk? I paid close to five hundred dollars for it but can't use it because it counter-indicates for my symptoms. It can accommodate a personal body weight of up to three hundred pounds and I'd be willing to let you have it for less. Make me an offer. (*Pause.*) Anti-gravity, Mr. Pronk. It decompresses the spinal column and takes pressure off those degenerative disks and irritated nerve endings. Medical science swears by it and so would I, if it didn't unaccountably cause me more harm than good. (*Pause.*) It's not that I'm not

self-aware. I'm highly self-aware. I've had seven years of therapy and know exactly where my red flags are. Stop fidgeting.

Pronk   Are you speaking to me?

Greever   I thought I was. Maybe I wasn't. (*PRONK reveals beads in hand.*) A rosary.

Pronk   Yes.

Greever   You're carrying a rosary. (*He stands.*)

Pronk   I look at this painting and don't see anything. It makes no sense. What comes to mind are memories. My father. His father. Me. My school tie. My hair combed. It's a jumble. Pictures from the past... if they'd just... And now they're gone. Just gone. And I think of my father, who's gone. And his father, who's gone. And the times I nearly died... and I thank God I'm still here because now I'm going to see my son. But I'm nervous. And I just don't have a good feeling.

Greever   Would you like me to check his flight status? (*She sits.*) Mr. Pronk? Would you like me to check his flight status?

(*PRONK turns to her. A young BOY appears in the open window behind GREEVER. PRONK stares at the BOY, who's dressed in a school tie with his hair neatly combed. GREEVER looks up from her computer.*)

Well, the Internet is down. The whole bloody system is crashed right down to the ground. We'll just have to wait and let the world sew itself back together. I'm a little loopy, I apologize. I've been in three time zones since last night. I'm sure he's fine. I'm sure he's beside himself with anxious excitement waiting to see his father. Take a breath, Mr. Pronk. Breathe deeply and discover everything is right where it should be. If we settle back far enough within ourselves, we find everything is waiting. Everything we think we've lost is right there and waiting. That's what I do when I think of... (*Pause. She angles herself slightly toward the boy, as though sensing him, then turns back to* PRONK.) But why the Philippines? Why the Philippines, Mr. Pronk? How interesting. You know, we launched that campaign in Manila last year. Pacific Telecom. Celebrating the power of analog communications to put people in touch with what counts.

(*She looks at* PRONK, *who remains transfixed on the* BOY, *until the* BOY *disappears. Lights down.*)

The End

The Diagnosis

by Coleman Hough

The Diagnosis *was presented by Sharon's Farm and Padua Playwrights at Bedlam Warehouse in Los Angeles, 2006, under the direction of Coleman Hough, with the following cast:*

WOMAN/ LINDA	*Christine Romeo*
DOCTOR WOMAN/MAGGIE	*Mary Greening*
DR. BESMAN	*David Weininger*

Setting

A dirty office. Some office furniture. In the rear are elevator doors.

(A WOMAN *waits alone in a dirty dark room. She hears strange noises coming from other rooms. Sex—laughter—surprise—pain. She tries to read but is distracted by the noise. Finally she puts her book down and presses her ear to the wall.*

DOCTOR WOMAN, *a woman in a white coat, comes in—she is focused on the contents of a chart. She sits down and reads intently, occasionally looking up and acknowledging the woman. But never with direct eye contact.)*

Woman   Are you Dr. Besman? I've heard so much about you and how you change lives—I went to this whole woman healthy woman seminar and everyone sang your praises. I feel honored to be here. It certainly is an unusual office. Plenty of parking though. I hate paying for parking. Parking on the street is just natural. It's where cars—

Doctor Woman   Let's be quiet for a moment.

Woman   Belong.

(They stare at each other. DOCTOR WOMAN *stands and circles* WOMAN.)

Doctor Woman   Lift your right arm.

Woman   This is the one that—

Doctor Woman   Now lift your left arm. Good job. Do you wake up feeling elated?

Woman	Not really no.
Doctor Woman	How long?
Woman	What?
Doctor Woman	How long has it been since your last elation?
Woman	About six weeks.
Doctor Woman	Was it full?
Woman	Yes.
Doctor Woman	And now?
Woman	Empty.
Doctor Woman	Is that the feeling?
Woman	I wake up feeling bitter.
Doctor Woman	Hmmmmmmmm.
Woman	Angry.
Doctor Woman	Huh.
Woman	There's evidence on my pillow.
Doctor Woman	What sort?
Woman	Stains. I have to turn the pillow over.
Doctor Woman	Interesting.
Woman	Sometimes I forget.
Doctor Woman	Are you forgetting things?
Woman	You mean like things?
Doctor Woman	Well, parts of your life?
Woman	The late eighties actually.
Doctor Woman	Consecutive years?
Woman	Like from May 1986 to the end of '90.
Doctor Woman	Does your scalp buzz?
Woman	Not really—no.
Doctor Woman	Do your hands and feet feel icy?
Woman	Warmish actually.
Doctor Woman	Warmish?

Woman	Well, warm.
Doctor Woman	Like a cake just cooling? Or a hand on your breast?
Woman	Hand on my breast.
Doctor Woman	And your legs?
Woman	Tense. I do yoga in the middle of the night.
Doctor Woman	Which pose?
Woman	Downward Dog is the only one I know the name of.
Doctor Woman	In the middle of the night?
Woman	Sometimes.
Doctor Woman	Ever during the day?
Woman	Always.
Doctor Woman	Where do you find the space?
Woman	Different places. Clean wide surfaces.
Doctor Woman	This is not normal.
Woman	What's wrong with me?
Doctor Woman	I'm not sure. I want to rule out stifled elation and faded memory—but it seems you have early onset rigor mortis.
Woman	What?
Doctor Woman	We have great drugs that will soften the process.
Woman	The process?
Doctor Woman	The flow.
Woman	What are my symptoms?
Doctor Woman	Forgetting almost half of an entire decade for one.
Woman	What kind of drugs?
Doctor Woman	Four years of faded memory is unusual.
Woman	If I really focus, I can—
Doctor Woman	Shhhhhhhhhhh.

(*During a long silence,* DOCTOR WOMAN *listens to the* WOMAN's *pulse. She starts humming "The Farmer in the Dell" to the beat of the pulse. Ascending in octaves and volume.*)
Mmmmmmm... mmmmmmm... mmmmmmm

(*The woman looks uncomfortable—terrified.* DR. BESMAN *comes into the room.*)

Dr. Besman   That's enough Maggie.

(*He is referring to* DOCTOR WOMAN, *who is silent. He turns to* WOMAN *and extends his hand.*)

    Doctor Besman.

Woman   Linda Price.

Maggie   She seems to have—

Dr. Besman   I'll make my own assessment. No one is at the front desk. Could you—

(MAGGIE *walks to the door—turns to* LINDA *and smiles. Winks. She takes the chart off the clipboard—tears it in half and lets the clipboard fall to the floor.*)

Linda   Was that—

Dr. Besman   Maggie's been with us a long time. She wants a promotion.

(He sits backwards in a chair opposite LINDA.*)*

Linda	I thought she was—
Dr. Besman	She's my warm up act.
Linda	Your—
Dr. Besman	Close your eyes.
Linda	What are you going to do?
Dr. Besman	Find you.
Linda	Oh.

*(*LINDA *closes her eyes.*)*

Did she go to medical school?

Dr. Besman	God no.
Linda	How does she—
Dr. Besman	Do you see anything?
Linda	Like—
Dr. Besman	Dots.
Linda	No.
Dr. Besman	Faces?
Linda	I always see faces.

*(*DR. BESMAN *stands up and yells.*)*

Dr. Besman	MAGGIE!!!!!!

*(*LINDA *opens her eyes—reaches down for her bag.*)*

Linda	I think I should—

Dr. Besman	If a building was badly water damaged say—do you see faces in the stains on the ceiling?
Linda	I—
Dr. Besman	Just yes or no.
Linda	Yes. I see two faces on my bedroom ceiling. One's in profile—the other is just an eye.
Dr. Besman	Maggie!

(*MAGGIE comes in the room.*)

Maggie	Your brother on three.
Dr. Besman	Does he sound out of breath?
Maggie	He always sounds out of breath.
Dr. Besman	(*To* LINDA.) I have a twin brother—identical, only he's an idiot.

(*He picks up the phone. LINDA smiles nervously at MAGGIE.*)

Yeah Tom... No don't use those they're flammable... That means they'll catch on fire... Use the ones to the left of—OK... (*To Maggie.*) He put me on hold "—the bastard's using my phone and he—Yeah, I'm with a patient... She's late thirties, early— (*To* LINDA.) Are you single? *To Tom* She looked away... Stop offending my patients.

(*LINDA gets up to leave. MAGGIE blocks the door. MAGGIE strong-arms her back to her chair.*)

Tom don't do this... Fish oil then... The vitamin B shots are for before bedtime... Just lock the door... Look, I've got to... Tomatoes and lemons, now leave me alone. Oh and there's basil in the—

(*He hangs up.*)

Linda   Garden?

Maggie   What did you want?

Dr. Besman   Get me psych form 273B—cognitive exam—notify Dr. Thomas—tell him that—

(*He whispers in* MAGGIE's *ear.* MAGGIE *nods and smiles at* LINDA.)

Thank you.

(MAGGIE *leaves and* DR. BESMAN *rolls his chair in close—face-to-face with* LINDA.)

Linda   I had a garden once—a whole acre of land. When I would weed the rows and rows of big boys, better boys—I would see flashes of darkness at the edge of the woods. A shape. I wanted to follow it—but knew it would follow me.

(DR. BESMAN *writes this down. Cocks his head.*)

Linda   Why am I telling you this?

Dr. Besman   I don't know. Go on.

Linda	Look, I need to be diagnosed.
Dr. Besman	With what?
Linda	Well, whatever it is I have so I can—
Dr. Besman	So you can—
Linda	So I—
Dr. Besman	So you can know what to expect.
Linda	Exactly.
Dr. Besman	So you can get the right control.
Linda	Yes—control.

(*DR. BESMAN and LINDA stare at each other for an awkward but connected silence. DR. BESMAN suddenly gets up—takes off his coat and walks to the door.*)

Dr. Besman	Then I can't help you.
Linda	But you're a doctor.
Dr. Besman	(*He yells.*) MAGGIE!
Linda	Don't y'all have a paging system here?
Dr. Besman	What did you say?
Linda	A paging system, you know, like Dr. Besman, line three is for you. It's Bob Dylan. Take a message.
Dr. Besman	I would probably take a call from Dylan.
Linda	It's an example—probably a bad one but—
Dr. Besman	I love Dylan. Worship that man. (*He stares out the window and hears a song in his head. He grooves to his own tune.*)
Linda	I want to be examined.
Dr. Besman	Uh-huh. (*He is still in a reverie of thought.*)
Linda	Tested.

(DR. BESMAN snaps to attention.)

Dr. Besman	It's a full time position. What else can you bring to the job?
Linda	The worst of myself.
Dr. Besman	Uh—
Linda	The best of myself. Look, I just want to know.
Dr. Besman	The truth right?
Linda	Right. The truth.
Dr. Besman	It's what's missing.
Linda	So let's get started.
Dr. Besman	Maggie!
Linda	Maybe she went to lunch.
Dr. Besman	Put your hands on your thighs—palms facing down—now up—down—up—good.
Linda	Now see? This feels important.
Dr. Besman	Touch your nose and follow my finger with your eyes. Touch my finger—excellent.
Linda	Connected.
Dr. Besman	Tap your foot as if you were hearing music.
Linda	Relevant, you know?
Dr. Besman	Now let's see you walk. Walk to the door and back.
Linda	Is this getting you closer to a diagnosis?
Dr. Besman	What was Maggie's diagnosis?
Linda	Isn't she the receptionist?
Dr. Besman	Sometimes she nails it. It unnerves me. That girl's got a gift.
Linda	She said I had early onset rigor mortis.
Dr. Besman	Good guess, we all do.
Linda	And that the process can be softened by drugs.

Dr. Besman	Good guess—everything can. I taught her all the tricks.
Linda	She figured it out. She's got it down. I like her but she talks too much.
D. Besman	We're all flawed, Linda. Maggie! We're all flawed and scarred and traumatized—we need more from relationships than we're willing to give. We're takers.

(*An elevator descends. The elevator doors open to reveal* MAGGIE.)

Dr. Besman	Now, take a deep breath. Give, Linda—Give yourself over to a higher power. Go limp. Relax. Surrender control. Let Maggie take you to where all will be revealed.
Linda	Where is that?
Dr. Besman	It's pleasant. You'll be surprised.
Linda	I need to pick up my—
Dr. Besman	Your son has already been picked up from violin. Your husband made dinner.
Linda	But he—
Dr. Besman	Shhhhhhhhhhh. Focus on your breath.
Linda	My husband's dead.
Dr. Besman	Surrender.

(*He nods to* MAGGIE. MAGGIE *picks* LINDA *up like a baby.* LINDA *goes limp.*)

Dr. Besman	That's it—Give, Linda—give over.

Linda   Am I being delivered for more testing?

(*MAGGIE steps onto the elevator with LINDA. The elevator doors close.*)

Dr. Besman   Delivered.

(*A scream is heard from the elevator. Black out.*)

The End

Pink

by Guy Zimmerman

Pink *was presented by Sharon's Farm and Padua Playwrights at Bedlam Warehouse, 2006, under the direction of the playwright, with the following cast:*

WALTER	*Mickey Swenson*
CLYDE	*Andrew Hopper*
ADELE	*Niamh McCormally*

Characters

WALTER   *The host of a right wing radio talk show.*
CLYDE   *A bartender at a nightclub.*
ADELE   *A demoness, formerly Walter's girlfriend.*

Setting

A bar at a nightclub.

(CLYDE, *behind the bar and* WALTER, *on a stool cheering and clapping for the previous act.*)

Walter	Wooo-hooo! Yeah! Yeah! Bravo!
	Woooooooo-hoooo!! (*He settles. A pause.*) Greetings, bar keep
Clyde	Hello, friend
	Enjoy the show?
Walter	Oh, sure 'Course I feel sorry for that one guy
Clyde	Goes without saying
Walter	I feel sorry for that one guy and I also feel sorry
	For that woman and for her mother
Clyde	Sometimes I think we push it too far
	How about you?
	Do you think we push it too far?
Walter	Oh, I wouldn't say that, no
Clyde	Well, I'm relieved to hear you say so
Walter	What Americans need more of is light-hearted entertainment
	America does not have enough light-hearted entertainment
	That's the whole problem with America
	Too little light-hearted entertainment

(*Pause.*)

	Perhaps you remember me
Clyde	I'll have to think on it, friend
Walter	I was in here six months back

	For that minstrel-type show you had with the gaff hooks
	Where we all had to wear those plastic smocks
Clyde	Wacky, right?
Walter	Wacky
	Yes it was
	The only part I didn't really care for was when that woman
	Turned that man into, like,
	A pet koala
Clyde	Oh, right
Walter	See, I didn't *buy* that
Clyde	And he shimmied up that pillar into the rafters
Walter	To me that wasn't *realistic*
	So I felt left out in the cold, see
	I mean, I couldn't quite get behind it
	You know, who am I *rooting* for?
Clyde	I heard those same comments many times
	Many times
Walter	I had a beautiful woman with me that night
	Only I didn't leave with her
	No I went home alone that night
	Left my woman friend sitting right there on that barstool
	She was deep in conversation
	With the barkeep
	That barkeep was you
Clyde	What'll it be tonight sir?
Walter	Tonight I'd like a Tanqueray martini
	Extra dry with olives

Clyde	Nice

(*CLYDE gets to work mixing the martini.*)

Walter	The name of the woman I was with
	Escapes me at the present time
	Although we were engaged to be married
Clyde	Adele was her name
Walter	Adele, correct
	To be honest when I brought Adele
	To your bar
	My secret hope was that she would meet someone
	Form a new attachment
	With all that entails
Clyde	I'm glad to hear that, sir
Walter	I had been told, in fact
	Ahead of time I had been told
	That this bar was just the place
	To bring a woman like Adele
Clyde	A woman who had become a... burden
Walter	A woman like Adele
Clyde	As you can see
	We do attract an international crowd

(*He serves the martini.*) Enjoy your drink, sir

(*WALTER sips. Savors. Gives CLYDE the thumbs up. Slams it back and silently orders another... and another.*)

Walter	Let's say I now
	Six months later, lets say I developed *concerns* and
	curiosity
	About Adele and what became of her
Clyde	Well...
Walter	And let's say I wanted to send her a message
Clyde	Oh sir that would hardly be possible
Walter	I see
Clyde	No no no
	It's best you leave the past behind you
	Sir
	Take my advice
Walter	Well, I thought I'd ask
Clyde	No harm done
Walter	I see these reports on *60 Minutes*
	About Nogales and Juarez and the women
	About Abu Dhabi and the women
	And remote Islands in the South China Seas
	And the high value of American women in
	particular
	And the terrible, truly terrible things...

(*Pause.*)

	Well, I certainly hope Adele is comfortable
	In her new situation
Clyde	Sir, those are five-dollar martinis
Walter	Oh, of course
	(*He pays. Settles.*)

See what happened is
The reason I came down here is
I found something of Adele's
Underneath the pillow I found it
A keepsake that belonged to Adele
(*Hesitates.*)
Well, here

(WALTER *pulls a small* PINK STUFFED POODLE *out of the inner pocket of his suit coat and places it on the bar.* CLYDE *recoils...*)

Clyde   Oh, sir...

Walter   I thought I got rid of all her stuff
But then about a week after I brought her in
That pink poodle showed up beneath the pillow
It's been laying around the apartment
Many times I've put it in the trash can
But then for some reason
I always take it out again
Put it in take it out
Put it in take it out
I stuffed it down the garbage disposal once
And then
You're gonna think this is a little odd
I heard the thing yapping
Thought I did anyway

Soft little yaps up from the drain in the bottom of the
sink
And now at night I wake up
I pretty much hear the damn thing yapping all
the time
Yapping softly underneath the fucking pillow

Clyde   Nothing worse than a yappy poodle

Walter   To be honest with you
That little stuffed dog is the source of all our
problems

Clyde   You and Adele?

Walter   The way she would talk to it
In this little baby voice
And she would comb it too with a little smile
And perfume it too, the pink fur

Lately I'll catch the fuckin' thing watching me too
Yapping little bitch of a lap dog
It's not even alive!
Fucking thing has *me* yapping
You think I'm joking?
I walk along, suddenly I fuckin' yap like a little
poodle
It's soft, under my breath, like
But literally
Yap yap yap
Like that
Yap yap yap yap

Mostly I can control it, but the other day during an interview

I work in radio, see

Got my own talk show on the radio, see

I start fucking yapping, couldn't stop, made a joke out of it, but still

(*Pause. Then, pointing...*)

I thought maybe you could get that to Adele

Wherever she is

It might, you know

Boost her spirits

Clyde   Well, to be honest with you

The place she's at now

That kind of keepsake

Isn't exactly all that appropriate

And I have to warn you

An object like that, a cherished object

A personal article of that sort has been known to accumulate

A kind of... *power*

What's the name?

Walter   The name of the poodle?

Clyde   Tell me the damn name...!

Walter   Pink

Is what she used to call it

Clyde   Pink, huh?

Walter   Pink, Pinkie, Pinka-doodle...

Clyde   I get the picture

Okay now

	Here's what I want you to do
	I want you to
	Drop Pink down
Walter	Down?
Clyde	Drop Pink down behind the goddamn bar...!

(WALTER *drops the poodle behind the bar. The men watch.* LIGHTS *shift and odd, disturbing sounds become audible behind the bar... After a moment,* ADELE *rises into view, materializing behind the bar, wearing a* PINK VEIL.)

Clyde	Oh, boy
Adele	Hello, Walter
Walter	Adele
Adele	Good evening, Clyde
Clyde	When I woke up this morning I knew
	That today was going to be one of those days
	Had me some dreams last night
	There was this lady in my dream, she was
	Floating above my head up near the rafters
	She was like
	Shitting out big sheets of pure liquid chocolate
	And the chocolate
	Dropped down onto my head
	And my head was made of something like crushed ice
	Like a snow cone
	Soaking up all that dark sweet nectar

	Oh, she was a complicated woman
	Very beautiful to the eye
	Good lord she was beautiful
	Dancing with her tambourine
	She had this tambourine it was made out of human skin
	And she had this big knife shaped like the moon
	Drinking all that blood
	My blood
	Your blood
Adele	Walter?
Walter	Yes?
Adele	Did you know that I'm going to have a baby?
Walter	I didn't know that, no
Adele	Yes, it's true
	Am I showing yet?
Walter	I think I see a little lump maybe
Adele	Motherhood is a form of addiction
	I'm looking forward to it
	Women go for that adulation
	We love the way those babies look up at us
	So helpless and pure
	Oh, I can feel him move
Walter	It's funny
Clyde	What's funny
Walter	I woke up today I was afraid
Clyde	Afraid of what?
Walter	Of demons
Clyde	What kind of demons?

Walter	The evil kind that it's hard to recognize
	Until after the fact
Adele	Are you afraid of me?
Walter	Yes
Adele	Have you always been afraid of me?
Walter	Yes
Adele	Look what I brought back with me
	From my trip
	(ADELE *holds up a leash and collar.*)
Walter	You don't need one of those!
Adele	No?
Walter	Not for Pink you don't!
Adele	Oh, it's not for Pink
Walter	Goddamn Pink is a fucking stuffed animal!
Adele	Stay perfectly still and this won't hurt at all

(ADELE *straps the collar around* WALTER's *neck. His arms come up in front of him like paws.*)

Walter	*Yap yap yap*
Clyde	Someone put crazy juice in your milk bottle, Mister
Walter	*Yap yap yap*

(WALTER *yaps more. Covers his mouth.* ADELE *leads* WALTER *around behind the bar.*)

| Clyde | Once she appears beside you |
| | There's no other way home |

She will drink you like water
It's gotta be seen to be believed
She will swallow you like smoke
You ask yourself
Why was I born just to suffer?
It's a good question
In some ways it is the *only* question
Perhaps you've heard about brother Satan
Well, brother Satan bows low when she steps near

(WALTER, *on his leash, descends out of view. Feeling tugs on the leash,* ADELE *descends out of view also.* CLYDE *polishes glasses.*)

She might hang down from the ceiling
Take a crap in your mouth
She's a yoga fanatic
Can you hear that distant music?
It's her special song—the last thing you'll ever hear
And I'll tell you the name of that song
"My pussy is a fucking shrine"
Is the name of that song
Remember it well:
"My... pussy... is... a... fucking... shrine..."

(LIGHTS *slowly fade as music rises as* CLYDE *serves a final, perfect martini.*)

The End

Numerology

by Cheryl Slean

Numerology *was presented by Sharon's Farm and Padua*
Playwrights at Bedlam Warehouse, 2006. It was directed by the
playwright with the following cast:

1   *Hugh Dane*
2   *Devon Carson*
3   *Mark Adair Rios*

Characters

1   *male.*
2   *female.*
3   *male.*

Setting

A big empty space with a roll-up or other large door opening to the outside.

(LIGHTS *up in a big open space. 1* (male) *leans against a wall, watching 2* (female) *pace anxiously. 1 has been there for a long time. 2 has arrived more recently.*)

2	They never tell you anything, that's the bitch of it.
1	Speak for yourself.
2	Send you somewhere, tell you to wait, tell you to eat and drink and wait, but there's nothing to eat and drink.
1	There's breadsticks.

(*He takes a breadstick from his pocket and sucks on it like a cigar.*)

2	That's not food, that's like turds at a bad party. A kid's party with punch.
1	But you wait.
2	Yeah, well I'm good at taking direction.
	(*1 snorts.*)
2	(*Defensive.*) What, I've been an actor.
1	I can tell when somebody's lying.
2	You? You're a big fat turd and a fag.
1	I'm a numerologist, too.
2	Oh, in addition?
1	You have a foul little mouth, they'll take that into account.
2	They?
1	*They* is a fact.
2	I hate that pronoun, so vague—*they* did this to me. *They* won't tell me why.
1	All language is imprecise. I prefer numbers—

2	Yeah, yeah—
1	—Everything in numbers. The sum of the parts and the parts of the whole. The individual, the universe, the convection between the two.
2	That doesn't bode well.
1	Give me your birthdate.
2	Why? Is it part of the *pact*?
1	Actually, yes.

(2 *looks him up and down.*)

2	God, look what you're wearing. You're either a fag or a pimp.
1	You undermine yourself—
2	Whatever—
1	—With your need to be cool, to avoid humiliation at all costs.
2	I'm not the only one.
1	It blocks you into a corner—
2	Huh!
1	—Undermines any serious study of life. Don't you see that?
2	(*Pause.*) I heard there were drinks around here. A bar upstairs or something.

(*She walks around looking unsuccessfully for stairs.*)

| 1 | Sure, self-medicate. |
| 2 | That phrase is full of shit and received wisdom. |

1	They say a drunk's always on the defensive.
2	Hey, I'm just busy avoiding humiliation over here.
	I mean Jesus, with everyone watching. (*Sarcastic—there's nobody watching.*)
1	Have a breadstick. (*He offers one, she ignores him.*) You want to drink cause you think too much.
2	Another gem, another gem. (*Pointing to her head.*) It's a thinking machine, stupid. You can't stop a thing's natural function. Tell me you can stop thinking, tell me that and I'll call you a liar.
1	The problem is not in the thinking per se, it's in the complete sublimation of reality to thought. Believing your thoughts are real, that's the problem.
2	Who do you think you are?
1	I'm the numerolog—
2	—Numbers, right. How is that not thinking? How is that not taking a thought, irrational as it may be, pathetic as it may be, and ascribing reality to it?
1	Not trying to win an argument here.
2	God forbid, you'd embarrass yourself. Is there nothing original about you at all?
1	Originality is a crapshoot. You hope your audience hasn't read the same books.
2	Audience, huh? What a dreamer.

(*3, male, enters, surprising 2.*)

3	Hi.
2	Hey! Where'd you come from?

(3 turns back and looks up doubtfully.)

3	Somewhere... um...
2	I heard there's a bar upstairs, is that true?
3	There's a lot of bars.
2	What's a lot?
3	Um, two?
2	Holy shit! Let's get up there.
3	No, I don't want to go back.
2	Why not?
3	*(Pause.)* I don't like to drink?
2	What?

(3 shrugs helplessly. 2 turns away in disgust.)

2	God, this country has gotten so straight. What happened to all the drinking and smoking? What happened to all the drugs?
1	They're still out there.
2	Yeah, among criminals. Losers and pregnant trailer trash and methamphetamine addicts. If you're older than twenty and middle class you're considered insane if you smoke. Everyone's so nice, so healthy, it makes me want to blow my brains out. The mundanity! The hypocritical liberal friendly niceness! Living clean for a healthier future, driving the fucking speed limit, buckling up, I mean give me a gun. *(To 3.)* Hey, do you think I can borrow your car?
3	I don't have a car.
2	You used to.
3	I did?

2	(*To* 1.) Did you tell me once this was hell? Stuck in a square room with a couple of straight shooters.
3	I think I'm an alcoholic.
2	Aw shit, don't tell me that.
3	My cross to bear.

(2 *walks away from the others, disgusted. 1 approaches* 3.)

1	What's your birthdate, friend?
3	People get kind of personal down here.
1	The personal and the universal. The limitless and the limit, the point and the plane, I could go on.
3	(*Re:* 1.) Does she know me? She acts like she knows me.
1	Let's see what the numbers say. When were you born?
3	I'm supposed to remember that, right?
1	The trip down the birth canal? Your mother's cries, the eggplant shape of your head? The first tickle of air on your skin. Strange, air. Everyone gathered round to stare, their faces flush with something, expectation. They stare at you so long you feel like a freak.
3	(*Blurting.*) August 4, 1970.
1	8, 4, 1970. 8 and 4 that's 12, add up to 3. 1, 9, 7 is 17, which is 8 plus 3 is 11, add up to 2. Two. (*Pause.*) There's an old folk tale that says the moon is made of green cheese. Green is the color of number-2 people who are indeed the children of the moon in her many moods. Twos are quick to adapt. But beware—they soak up others' thoughts and ideas until they start to forget things. Who they are, for example. Who they were or maybe could be, number 2? Beware of the chameleon.

3	That's weird.
1	Sound like someone you know?
3	But I made up the date, it's not mine.
1	It's yours.
3	I'm just saying I think you got lucky. You saw the look in my eyes, and you guessed.
1	No such thing as luck. It's all in the way the numbers resonate with the orbiting planets.
3	Not to be impolite, but that's pretty dumb.
1	People always trying to squeeze out of something.

(*2 suddenly cries out.*)

2	Oh, god, why! Why'd I have to end up in this thing? This crap tube, this tomb for the soul.

(*2 approaches the others in despair. 3 offers a breadstick. 2 takes it disconsolately.*)

1	Don't worry, not too much longer.
2	How do you know?—Never mind.
1	To be a good numerologist, you have to be friendly with time.
2	Time? Time? Time is a concept.
1	Who's unoriginal now.
2	I have a headache. I think I'm losing my mind.
1	Time and the planets circling...
3	Maybe it's all starting over. Repeating itself, have you noticed? Always the same party, the same people, with different outfits. And everyone's standing around, you

know, thinking their own experiences are more
interesting than everyone else's, except everyone else is
thinking that too, so the talk just keeps getting louder,
people trying to outdo each other in comedy and pathos,
I like *this*, I think *that*, madly defining themselves, madly
jabbing finger to chest, but no one is even listening,
they're just waiting for their turn to talk, so they have to
yell even louder, until finally everyone's screaming,
jumping up and down and screaming—mee, mee, look at
meeeeeee!

(*The others stare. 3 rubs his temples.*)

3   I'm so tired. I'm tired.

(*1 pats his back congenially. Then walks off, checking a
pocket watch. 2 goes to 3.*)

3   He said my head was shaped like an eggplant.
2   So?
3   I have a headache.
2   *I* have a headache.
3   Well, we can both have headaches.

(*3 watches suspiciously as 1 goes about some business.*)

2   Never mind him, he's a charlatan. He thinks he knows
more than he should, like he thinks he's Prometheus or
something. But he's just another dumb cat in the big
black bag of the world.

3	Why do you talk like that?
2	Come on man, you can take it. You're an addict, right? I bet you got stories.

(*2 jabs 3 congenially on the shoulder.*)

3	I can't remember.
2	Come on. The story's the best part of the meeting. (*She jabs him again.*)
3	I told you, I can't!
2	Putz.
3	My mind's gone blank or something, like when you're trying to think of a word and you can't, and you know it was in there once, you remember remembering the word, but the word itself—Gone into this hole, this empty spot. And it's always the same word, have you noticed?
2	(*Re:* 1.) What's he doing over there?
3	You would think the sheer repetition of forgetting it over and over should help you remember the next time, but no...

(*At the far end of the space,* 1 *pushes a button, causing a tall door at the end of the room to start rolling up, revealing the world outside.*)

... once again you forget.

2	Holy shit!

(*2 rushes to the door. She kneels and peers through the opening as it widens. She jumps up and gestures to 3.*)

| 2 | Hey, come here! Check this out! |

(*3 sighs and approaches the door.*)

	Lookie, look! It's night-time. Sweet!
1	ONE.
2	I see some lights out there. Is it a city?
1	TWO.

(*2 clutches her head in pain, and immediately after, 3 clutches his.*)

2	Shit! My head!
3	Ah!
1	Not much longer. THREE.
3	I feel cold coming in.
2	What? It's balmy! Christ, what a baby.
3	You're the baby.
1	FOUR.
2	(*Staring out the door.*) Wait a minute. What *is* this?
1	FIVE.
2	Is this L.A.?
1	It's L.A.?
2	We're still in fucking L.A.?
3	I told you—the same thing starting over.

(*The door comes to a halt, fully open. 2 and 3 look out.*)

2	It's like a magnetic force, L.A. You think you got out of town two hours ago and you look around and for chrissake you're still in it.
3	Because it's so big. It's endless.
2	Endless. (*Clutching her head.*) God, what a nightmare.
1	Not much longer. SIX.
3	(*To 2.*) Whatsa matter, you scared of the city?
2	Look at it. It's like a goddamn kid's birthday party out there!
3	Aw, she's scared. Don't be scared honey, it's only the clown. (*He yells in her face.*) L.A.! The movies! (*Laughing, turning to 1.*) Hey numbers, you wanna make a movie?
2	Oh no... not another movie.

(*2 shrinks back in horror from the door. 1 stops her with his arm.*)

| 1 | SEVEN. |

(*2 looks at 1 in alarm.*)

| 2 | What are you doing? |

(*1 pushes her back toward the door, where 3 grabs her by the elbow.*)

| 3 | And this girl right here could be our star. |

(3 *pulls 2 closer to the door.*)

2   Let go!

3   Wouldn't she make a good star?

1   EIGHT.

3   Hey listen, don't worry, you'll like it. Everyone treats you
      special, like you're the only girl in the world. Pretty,
      elastic skin, center of attention. For a while, anyway—

2   Let me go!

3   Till you grow up, get old, get sick, till the skin becomes
      less elastic, and the doors begin to shut, and all the
      people stop calling, and you're living out your stupid life
      from the corner of a dark little room.

1   (*To 3.*) Damn, boy, you got mean.

2   (*To 3.*) Leave me alone! (*To 1.*) Tell him I don't want to go.

1   Always the smart ones. Thinking they have a choice.

(3 *starts to laugh at the joke he assumes is at 2's
expense.*)

What are *you* laughing at?

(1 *has moved behind both of them now. 3 sees and
abruptly stops laughing.*)

3   Oh, shi—

1   NINE.

(1 *shoves both 2 and 3 out the door. They stumble out a
few steps and stand there, frozen.*)

112

1   (*Looking out at 2 and 3*). Three and three, that's good!
    Oh that's nice, that's symmetrical. Not that it'll help
    them much.
    (*He pushes the button to start the door rolling down. He
    takes out a breadstick and smells it like a cigar.*)
1   But anyway. Back to one.

(*1 exits nonchalantly, eating the breadstick. Outside, 2
and 3 consider their surroundings fearfully. 2 turns and
starts back to the door, a look of utter terror on her
face. After a few steps she stops. She doesn't know
where she is going. 3 gently takes her by the arm. They
walk off, together, slowly. The door clangs shut.*)

The End

Snakes and Ladders

by Kevin O'Sullivan

Snakes and Ladders *was presented by Sharon's Farm in an office in Santa Monica, 2007, under the direction of Kevin O'Sullivan, with the following cast:*

ROYCE   *Mickey Swensen*
WILSON   *Gill Gayle*

Characters

ROYCE   *An alpha-male in a power suit.*

WILSON   *A disheveled street-person with grubby beard.*

Setting

Office. Floor-to-ceiling windows. A row of identical cubicles.

(ROYCE, *Alpha male in a power suit, stands before window. Sitting on the floor, a disheveled street-person, WILSON. Between them, a gasoline can. ROYCE gestures to something beyond the window.*)

Royce   The boats have come unloosed from their moorings. Those people out there—what do they hope to accomplish? All day long. No one forced them to invest their pensions. This all started—right here. (*Taps head.*) I incubated it, in my brain. I built this place. Muscle and sinew. I am this place. Those people out there—it's me they're hurting. It's my flesh that's ripped. They won't be happy until they have my head in a basket. Don't they know I'm already a dead man? (*Beat.*) What's it like, to lose everything?

Wilson   You can't. There's always something left. Clings to you. Like a memory. There's too much to forget. The past gets smaller but it doesn't go away. You try to make your existence small with shallow breaths. You remember things. Your dog. Your dad. You remember they're both dead and it makes you... sad. People come to you in dreams. White poppies. River of snakes. The dead remind you you're alive. You try not to think and that's OK but you still remember. Even if the memories are wrong. Maybe your dog isn't dead. It's possible. (*Beat.*) If you make yourself quiet, shut everything else out, you can hear whispers on the other side. It's my observation that the dead speak in soft voices.

Royce   Do you believe in karma? I went out with a girl, she was
always talking how your karma catches up with you.
Good or bad. You mean right away, I asked. This life or
the next, she said. She believed all that shit, that we have
many lives. Said she could remember some of hers. I was
never going to wait for karma to make things happen.
Anything good, anything bad, I'm responsible for it. I
know exactly why it happens the way it does. A mistake
is a mistake. And luck is a matter of odds. I thought that.
Until now. Because it's not all clear to me. All this
happening. I can see certain things, things that lead
up—but this, what it's come to—why? How did it come
to this? Is this some sort of karma? I'm up to my chin in
shit. With each breath I inhale this odor. I'm stuck,
mired in it, and it's suffocating.

Wilson   I was a coward when I had to fight. Because I had to
know I exist. I needed proof. I lacerated my flesh until
my substance leaked red from my wounds, pain my
proof, but to exist is not to be. No being without
witness—this awful dependence—hence the struggle.
You are not a fact. You are a perception.

Royce   Pigs wallow in shit but I'm not a pig. I'm not supposed to
be, but that's what I am, 'cause right now I don't deserve
this. Try convincing them but—it's not my fault. Not
this time. This time it's not my fault. So it must be for
something else. (*Beat.*) And here I am looking at crap
I don't believe, trying to find an answer.

Wilson   I was in India. Calcutta. Delhi. I rode the train. I saw their
holy river, the Ganges. Human waste and bodies floating

in it. The dead are everywhere. I was sick most of the time
I was there. I couldn't leave my hotel room for a week. On
the streets you step over dead bodies, covered with flies.
I remember the smell of cow shit, diesel, and decay. When
I got better I went for a walk. There was a crowd on one
side of the street, surrounding this man who had just died.
His eyes were still open. He wasn't that old. I was nineteen
at the time and he wasn't much older than me. A fly kept
landing on his eye, like it was licking the moisture that
was left. Then people started scattering rupees. On his
body. I asked what that was for and I was told to pay the
people who take away his body. Then someone started
scattering bird seed, sprinkling it in his hair, on his face
and chest. When I asked about that I was told the seeds
were to pay the birds to take his soul away.

Royce   Who has dignity? Does anyone get the concept?

Wilson   Another lost language, dead with no one left to speak it.

Royce   What you see is groveling. Grovelers abound. No dignity
              there! No self-respect.

Wilson   Words have come unhinged: they can neither shut out
              nor let in.

Royce   People grovel so much their backs are stooped.

Wilson   Words have no substance, therefore they are vapor.

Royce   We'll wind up on all fours one day, back where we
              began. Evolution will make it easier to grovel. Even the
              monkeys will laugh at us. They'll be the ones standing
              tall. While we go back to grubbing, turning the earth
              with our snouts, gobbling up squirming insects. That's
              where all this leads, this groveling. Straight to grubbing.
              Those who specialize in brown-nosing will develop

longer snouts, the better to stick up some ass, and when they're not doing that they'll be fighting with anteaters over termite mounds. Do you agree, Wilson?

Wilson If we could let go of our bodies that would be a good thing.

Royce That's where this is all going. That's our destiny, if the world doesn't end soon, if we don't destroy it. And that's the proof there is no God because if there were he'd have pulled the plug on this a long time ago. If there is a God he walked away from his fuck-up. He's certainly not paying attention unless he finds colossal failure amusing.

Wilson We make these forts to protect our egos, keep everything else out—the truth. We are trapped in them, it keeps our illusions alive, the illusion that we actually exist. (*Beat.*) That's why I'm going to starve myself, loosen the bricks of my prison. When I escape from myself, I'll be free.

Royce They want to bury me but I won't let them. Let them sift through the ashes. You are my witness. You understand. What I have to do. Fuck the consequences. (*Beat.*) I want to be cremated. Right here. I need you to explain.

Wilson I am a free man.

(*WILSON grabs gas can from ROYCE pours its contents—a mere few drops—onto his head. WILSON tries to strike a match from a wet matchbook, without success.*)

Royce ... drifting... directionless... This is my ship and I am its captain.

The End

The Advantages of a Steep Roof

by Susan Hayden

The Advantages of a Steep Roof *was one of twelve short plays chosen in a nationwide competition for Collision Festival West and produced by Regroup Theatre in collaboration with the Ruskin Group Theatre at the Ruskin Group Theatre in Santa Monica, starring Paul Linke as Sid and Casey Kramer as Goldie.*

> *Now laughing friends deride,*
> *Tears I cannot hide,*
> *So I smile and say, when a lovely flame dies,*
> *Smoke gets in your eyes,*
> *Smoke gets in your eyes.*

—Jerome Kern & Otto Harbach

Characters

SID   *A more-than-middle-aged, low-budget zhlub in polyester*
Sansabelt pants and patent leather loafers.

GOLDIE   *An overly made-up West-West Valley divorcee.*

Setting

A suburban street in Thousand Oaks, CA. Three A.M.

(SID is sitting behind the wheel of his parked, 1970-ish Cadillac Coupe de Ville with GOLDIE, who's had one too many mini-bottles of Inglenook tonight. The song, "Smoke Gets In Your Eyes," sung by the Platters, plays in the background. A siren sounds in the distance.)

Goldie	Candy-ass.
Sid	Huh?
Goldie	You're a candy-ass.
Sid	Excuse me?
Goldie	Haven't you ever heard of The Rock, former professional wrestler? *(She does her best imitation.)* "The Rock is going to get out there tonight and do what he does best, and that's lay the smackdown on your roody-poo candy-ass!"
Sid	I'm not a wrestler but I do consider myself a professional.
Goldie	Yeah, a real professional. You're a candy-ass used car salesman.
Sid	I'm in the automotive trade. I sell previously owned cars. Got a problem with that?
Goldie	You're a candy-ass used car salesman with no college degree.
Sid	That's never stopped Sid Rose from anything.
Goldie	An uneducated, roody-poo candy-ass, former department store coin dealer.
Sid	Numismatist. I was a numismatist at Robinsons before it merged with the May Company.
Goldie	You keep your coins in a Mason jar.
Sid	That's my savings. My fuck-you money.

Goldie	You live in a bachelor apartment. A furnished single with a Murphy bed, hot plate, and multi-colored shag rug.
Sid	I got a lovely place. It's a conversion. Don't knock it.
Goldie	You go to Fromin's for the early-bird special, you still roll coins and you use coupons on dates. You're one step up from being a transient.
Sid	(*He reaches into his pants.*) Here, you want my balls, just take 'em, Goldie.
Goldie	Your point of view: minuscule. You won't take a chance. You don't see the big picture.
Sid	I'm a simplified man, Goldie. I see... what's in front of me.
Goldie	Oh really? Then why don't you drive closer, so I can see it too?
Sid	(*Pause.*) Everyone knows you can't get closer than five hundred feet. That's why there's The Law. We're already at the fifty-foot mark.
Goldie	What are they going to do, arrest us?

(*He shrugs.*)

Sid, if you re-start the car and turn right on that cul-de-sac over there, go up that hill off the dirt road, and hide the car behind those dumpsters, we'll have an aerial view.

Sid	And if I smoke a pack a day for the next twenty years, I'll get cancer. Big shocker.
Goldie	I want you to gun it. Gun it!

Sid	Fat chance. If you want to watch, it'll have to be from here.
Goldie	This is sooo boring! What are you afraid of? Think you'll get burned?
Sid	That's it. I'm starting the car and turning around. We're out of here. This date is over.
Goldie	Please wait. We can stay put. (*She pulls out her lipstick, shifts the rear-view mirror in her direction.*) Just take it in. (*Sighing.*) This is so much better than a drive-in movie.
Sid	Thrill of the hunt. It's passé for people our age. And *gauche*. Very *gauche*. Don't you know that, Goldie?
Goldie	I'm into the element of surprise, Sid. I'm into heart palpitations, at any cost.
Sid	Firebugs are warped people. With nothing better to do…
Goldie	I'm not a bug. Don't call me names!

(*The siren sounds again, this time, closer.*)

Sid	You should talk. Let's get one thing straight. I'm no "roody-poo candy-ass."
Goldie	Prove it.
Sid	You think you're so hip with your danger-chasing ways. Well lemme tell you something, I know risk. I've been with risky women. I had a woman who'd shaved her bush into a swastika—her ex was a Nazi sympathizer—and after her, there was one who used her hands on me like a Braun food processor—choppy, but in a *productive* way.
Goldie	Big wow, thanks for turning me on. (*She's restless in her seat, trying to get a better look.*)

Sid	My last true love married her father by mistake, and they had these freaky kids who all played the left-handed banjo.
Goldie	Stop. Stop talking. Now. Dim bulb. No spark.
Sid	… Once I dated a pet groomer. She herself looked like a standard poodle: curly pigtails, rhinestone collar, the inimitable fragrance that only comes from special doggy shampoo.
Goldie	And you wonder why I like doing these kinds of things with you? What the hell else is there to do? You're a snooze-fest, Sid.
Sid	I've been with *thousands* of women. Millions. I can't believe I didn't get AIDS in the '80s. I was the only one not using a condom back then.
Goldie	Great. So now, on top of being with a candy-ass, I'm HIV positive. Thanks. Thanks a lot.
Sid	When I was in my mid-thirties, I dated a woman roofer. She taught me a lot about protective coating, shingles, scaffolding. She climbed to the tops of homes, took me with her one time. She was always clean, never dusty. Smelled like a bed of roses. Used this deodorant spray on the backs of her thighs. *Diorissimo* or some goddamned thing. She herself fell thirty feet off a smoke stack and had to walk on crutches for life. Crushed her spine. Now *she* was good people. She knew about real danger, not watching it from a distance. She was in the thick of it.
Goldie	Quit while you're ahead, Sid.
Sid	Did you know there are advantages to a steep roof? It's true. They shed more water and create space.

Goldie	All the better for jumping off. Which is what I feel like doing at this very moment.
Sid	Lemme make myself Windex-clear. I've seen all kinds of women, in every state of dress and undress you can imagine. I've done it in phone booths, driveways, even on Ventura Boulevard, in broad daylight, once. But these days, at my age, I'm not into cheap thrills.
Goldie	If you had more spunk in the bedroom department, maybe I wouldn't need cheap thrills.
Sid	You're the first to complain.
Goldie	Oh, really? Well I have a confession to make. I'm feeling attracted to other men, I'm having uncontrollable feelings of attraction to the men in your life, like your brother in law, your niece's husband, your boss. I can't even be around them. In the right place, at the right moment, I'd be weak. I want to fuck them all.
Sid	Jesus Christ.
Goldie	Truth is, I'm not attracted to you anymore. I haven't been, for about a year.
Sid	We've only been goin' together for a year-and-a-half.
Goldie	You're an empty shell. A can of Tab. A cap gun.
Sid	I'm not the one who wears a full face of make-up to bed every night. I'm a man of high honor and self-esteem. Now honor… that's something you earn. It doesn't matter what your job is, how much you got in the bank. It's how you see the world and how you act in it. To others.
Goldie	(*Ignoring him as the sounds of crackling fire and sirens build*.) Start the car and drive a few more feet closer to it. I beg of you. I want to feel the heat against my skin.

130

I want to cough 'til I can't breathe. I want to see something burning.

Sid This is so sick. Can't you think of anything better to do than watch a goddamn fire?

Goldie No, I can't. I really can't.

Sid Someone's house is burning down: their belongings, family pictures, mementos—those things you can't get back. Finito. And you want the charge of watching it all turn to ash.

Goldie Wait! Do you see something? I think I see the flames! (*She reaches into her purse, takes out her cell phone, rolls down the window, leans out and starts taking pictures of the fire.*)

Sid (*Choking from the smoke that's just come through the window.*) What're ya, nuts? I can't breathe. I used to be OK with smoke in my lungs 'cuz I knew you liked it. But this... this is starting to remind me of being in the army, when they'd tell us to take off our gas masks.

Goldie Oh my God, this is amazing. (*She melts into what she is feeling.*)

Sid Goldie, I have a confession to make. I did this. For you. I started this fire. What choice did I have? I couldn't bear another night of name-calling, jabs and insults. I thought if I took charge, we'd be able to salvage something of this so-called domestic partnership.

Goldie What? You did this... for *moi*?

Sid Outside my condo, the ground was dry in that way it could only be on a hot August night in Thousand Oaks. I thought of Neil Diamond. I thought of you.

I remembered how, at camp in the Catskills, we learned how to start a fire with a can of coke and a bar of chocolate, no shit. Toblerone won't work, but Hershey's will. You polish the bottom of the can with the chocolate and create a reflector, a mirror finish. I felt inspired.

Goldie You risked your life?! Your future? Oh, Sid. You could get arrested. For arson!

(*She starts breathing heavily, begins to unbutton her blouse and take off her clothes, reaches for him and they passionately embrace.*)

You are *so hot.*

(*The sound of* FIRE *builds to deafening. As they make out, the car becomes engulfed in smoke. There is the sound of sirens.*)

The End

Knots

by Heidi Darchuk

Knots *was produced by Padua Playwrights as part of* A Thousand Words *at ArtShare L.A., 2008, under the direction of Gill Gayle, with the following cast:*

WRECK	*Lisa Denke Littman*
CAPTAIN	*Mickey Swenson*
JETT	*Lake Sharp/ Nicole Disson*
ANNE	*Caroline Duncan*
PEGBOY	*Jack Littman*
THE STARS	*Alisha Beth Adams*

Characters

THE WRECK   *Female, a beautiful, decaying vessel.*
CAPTAIN   *Male, adrift.*
JETT   *A mermaid in a wheel-chair.*
ANNE   *A lady pirate of the Carolinas.*
PEGBOY   *A slave.*

Setting

At sea.

(*THE* WRECK *faces the horizon.*)

Wreck Do you want to live forever? Take a look. My peeling face, my broken bottom. Everything enters. Everything pushes in. Water has ruined me. He was gentle yet firm. He stayed his course, through storms and darkening waters, measuring the stars until... there were no stars. Disaster, and what did the captain do? He jumped. There has been time and there will be more time. There will be time until the end. He will die if he's not dead already.

(*An accordion plays. Somewhere in the ocean, the* CAPTAIN *makes his way to the end of his rope.*)

Captain Bait loop, barrel hitch, beer knot, boom hitch, bottle sling, bowline on a bight...

Wreck Dead reckoning is navigation without stellar observation.

Captain Carrick bend, catshank, chain stitch, clove hitch, common whipping, continuous ring hitching...

Wreck The length of a nautical mile is almost identical to a minute of latitude.

Captain I used the sea for many years. I lost not a minute of time, but pursued my purpose.

Wreck My name, before I was called The Wreck, Sinthome is a French name.

Captain On the coast of St. Thomas we met with a vessel full of rum, which we were in great want of.

Wreck Always in great want of what we do not have. Ruled by our nots.

Captain	Diagonal lashing, diamond knot, dog shank, double Windsor (for use in neckties), dropper loop, egg loop,
Wreck	The words do not belong to us.
Captain	European death knot, eye splice.
Wreck	It slips down.
Captain	Fortune that had hitherto been so prosperious to us has left her minions and baffled for the present all my hopes.
Wreck	The real, the symbolic and the imaginary bind together. What keeps things in place is the name of the father.
Jett/Captain	There are no stars.

(*On a nearby vessel,* ANNE PEGBOY, *and* JETT *sit at a table wearing party hats.*)

Anne	Forget it, kid. He's not going to show. Captains. Fathers.
Jett	I know he's trying. Let's just wait a few more minutes.

(*They wait.*)

Wreck	Time and space are approximations.

(*And wait.*)

Anne	To a captain, the front and the back of a woman look exactly the same.
Jett	People carve pieces out of each other. They don't add anything.
Anne	He's probably fucking a waitress somewhere.
Jett	They make wreckage. And then flowers grow out of the burnt spaces.

Anne	If you add a lot of shit they do. Ha ha ha. Pegboy!

(PEGBOY *jumps up.*)

Anne/Captain

	A bottle of rum!
Captain	I drink, therefore I am.
Jett	That's the kind of guy you want.
Anne	Pegboy?
Jett	He's always doing sweet stuff for you.
Anne	He can't steer a ship, but he does alright.
Jett	Do you, um, pay him?
Anne	I raided a wussy little outfit called The Bachelor. A huge score, but I lost a score of men. It was a sick battle, even for... Anne! Arms and heads floating in the water. Grown men strangled with their own intestines. Pegboy, here was chained up in the galley. Seems since he was smooth and pretty, they'd keep him around for, you know—I left the ship with plunder *and* booty. So he's an indentured servant, only I don't think he minds.

(PEGBOY *returns with a bottle.*)

Anne	To Jett, the saddest, loveliest, most fair ladyfish in a wheelchair!

(*They drink.*)

Captain	Miller's knot, monkey's fist!

138

Wreck	Failure can be defined as the knot moving relative to the object being gripped.
Captain	Sheepshank, sheetbend, slipknot...
Anne	How do you like yer gift?
Jett	What gift?
Anne	Starts with a peg and ends with a boy!
Jett	I don't want a slave!
Anne	Sure ya do. Someone to fetch yer rum and push yer chair, oil yer scales.
Jett	This is embarrassing...
Anne	Don't worry. I'll get another.

(PEGBOY *plays the accordion. The* CAPTAIN *sings a sea shanty.*)

Captain	A handsome young seaman lay dyin',
	And as on the foredeck he lay,
	To around him his comrades come sighin',
	These last mournful words he did say:

Wrap me up in my tarpaulin jacket
And say a poor buffer's laid low;
Send for six salty seamen to carry me
With steps mournful, solemn and slow.

(PEGBOY *does a jig. The stars come out.*)

Had I the wings of a little dove,
So high on my pinions I'd fly.
Slap bang to the heart of my bonnie love,

And there I would stay til I die.

Wrap me up in my tarpaulin jacket
And say a poor buffer's laid low;
Send for six salty seamen to carry me
With steps mournful, solemn and slow.

(*The* CAPTAIN'*s rope finally leads him to The Wreck.*)

Captain	Sinthome!
Wreck	I'm called the Wreck, now.
Captain	Sinthome. Sinthome.
Wreck	Man over!
Captain	You were sinking, if I've got it straight.
Wreck	I sank alone.
Captain	There were slaves!
Wreck	Slaves can't steer!
Captain	Dead reckoning is navigation without stellar observation. If there's cloud cover. If yer blind drunk—
Wreck	A captain stays his course.
Captain	The stars decide. You are...
Wreck	Ruined.
Captain	Yer still a handsome vessel.

(*He leans in to embrace her.*)

Wreck	You need shelter and you're afraid. You left something you want.
Captain	Silver cups. Jerkied meat. Feather bed?
Wreck	There's nothing left.

Captain	Jett?
Wreck	She thinks you're dead.
Anne	I could find him and kill him.
Jett	If he's not dead already...
Anne	I could do it alone, but if you wanted to help...
Jett	He's not coming.
Anne	Snuff out the spirit.
Jett	How many have you killed?
Anne	Does it matter? Hundreds! This is it, Jett. We live and then we die.
Jett	Once upon a time, there was a yellow cake, the sun was shining, that kind of day. My mother ran out of butter for the frosting so she walked down to the corner store. I was in the front yard cutting jasmine. She asked me to do it but I didn't want to—!
Wreck	Quickly!
Jett	She said.
Wreck	The flowers are already falling, shrinking. There's not enough time.
Jett	She was hit by a car right in front of our house on my birthday. It started to rain. It rained for hours until the hours turned into years. It rained until there was no dry ground. Either you learn to sail or learn to swim. It's my birthday and he promised.
Captain	I'll stay on land as long I'm able.
Wreck	The words, they don't belong to us.

(*He puts his rope around her. Ties it.*)

| Jett | Why doesn't *he* ever say anything? |

| Anne | Pegboy? |
| Jett | Can you speak? |

(PEGBOY *opens his mouth and the* CAPTAIN *blows in.* ANNE *puts her hand on her sword.*)

Anne	Look what the nets dragged in!
Jett	Poppa?
Captain	My sweet lil' Jetty.
Anne	Pegboy, A round!
Captain	I've got something for ya on Saturn's return.

(*He gives her a box.*)

| Anne | Fancy. |

(JETT *opens the box and finds a pair of high heeled shoes.* ANNE *draws her sword.*)

| Captain | Ha Ha ha. Shoes to a mermaid! |

(*They laugh.* THE WRECK *blooms jasmine.*)

| Jett | Can you smell it, poppa? It's the night blooming kind. |
| Pegboy | Soon... |

(*They look at him.*)

It will be over.

The End

All Around the World

by Michael Hacker

All Around the World *was presented by Sharon's Farm, Folly Bowl,*
2009, under the direction of the playwright, with the following cast:

ELIAS	*Mark Fite*
ECHO	*Rachel Whitman*
EL PATRON	*Gray Palmer*

(*ELIAS enters carrying a large flashlight. He shines the light, looking around.*)

Elias   This place is a piece of shit.

(*ECHO enters.*)

This is private property.

Echo   I don't know what it is.

Elias   It's private property.

Echo   But you're not the owner.

Elias   I'm here on his business. And I'll tell you what. This is not what I expected. Not by a long shot. If I didn't have GPS in the rental I wouldn't even believe this is the right place. But it matched up perfectly with the address. What are you doing here?

Echo   I'm working out.

Elias   You're exercising.

Echo   I'm practicing.

Elias   Why do they call this place "The Orphan?"

Echo   I've never seen anyone else here until now. I don't know any details, nothing like what this place is, or what it's called.

Elias   According to El Patron, it's called The Orphan.

Echo   It's quiet and out of the sun. I come here every day.

(*ELIAS pulls out a phone and turns it on. He studies the display, thinks about making a call, then puts it away.*)

Elias	There will be a thousand hot hells to pay if I don't have the goods. And believe you me, I do not have the goods.
	(ELIAS *unhitches a large tape measure from his belt.*)
	I need something to record measurements.
Echo	Of what?
Elias	Of this... whatever this is.
Echo	Go ahead.
Elias	Go ahead and what?
Echo	Go ahead and measure. I have perfect recall.

(*He looks at her. He looks at the tape measure. He stretches out the tape.*)

Elias	Sixteen.

(*ECHO nods. ELIAS stretches the tape in another direction.*)

Nine and three-quarters.

(*ECHO nods. ELIAS tries to stretch the tape out again but it gets all tangled up.*)

This is bullshit. (*Pause.*) I have no idea what the fuck I'm doing. El Patron is on his way. He could show up tonight, tomorrow, in five minutes. I have no way of pinning it down more exactly. The exact time doesn't even matter. He's a cruel taskmaster. A martinet, you understand?

Echo	You remind me of a midget I used to know.

Elias	What?
Echo	You're taller. But you have the same mannerisms.
Elias	Look. I'm going to level with you. I drove in last night, I don't know a soul here, I can't find my way around, and I can't understand what I'm seeing out there. It's not a city like other cities I've seen.
Echo	(*She points.*) The city is there, and there is the valley. They have little in common. The valley is hard and bright, and the city is soft and dull. A person going from one to the other transforms. A sweaty plumber in the city becomes a leggy schoolteacher in the valley.
Elias	I don't see anyone working. Everyone is eating or driving or sending messages. Sometimes all three at once.
Echo	People here put a big stake in positive thinking.
Elias	Never served me. I used to work in a poison factory. Marketing. Wrote copy. I wasn't allowed to repeat words. If I repeated a word, or strayed into certain subjects, my computer shut down. But some words need repeating. Some words have no synonym. After awhile I stopped writing completely. I would find things by other people and copy them, like a third grader who forgot to study for the test. Turns out my computer was rigged to send subsonic messages filled with terrifying content. I had no idea what was happening and just continued getting more and more anxious. Anxious and depressed. It was a bad time.
Echo	I worked in the circus. I was a flyer.
Elias	Really?
Echo	It was a family run deal. Not my family. Circus folk. That's a particular breed. I got a job selling souvenirs and when they moved on I stayed with them, that's how

it started. I liked seeing new places and the money was as good as I could make at home.

Elias El Patron pays my salary. No benefits but cash on the barrel head every two weeks and he's never late. When I say 'he' I'm talking about the corporation or whatever entity he employs to take care of his business. Or maybe there is no corporation. Maybe it's just him. Just El Patron, in complete control of his entire empire. Which is far-flung. And we're standing on what might be the most far-flung corner of his entire universe. And I lied to him.

Echo What do you do for him?

Elias I'm supposed to handle the western territory. I rarely see El Patron himself. As a matter of fact, I've never seen him. But I've certainly felt his presence. I've talked to him on the phone. In point of fact I haven't actually spoken to him on the phone but I've received messages from him. I have no idea what he looks like except the pictures that flash in my mind when I'm thinking about him or getting messages from him. But all this isn't leading up to some hocus-pocus about how he may or may not be real. He's real, alright? And I lied to him. I said I'd covered The Orphan and had all the specs and was writing up a report with recommendations and all the rest. You don't know the specs on this place, do you?

Echo No.

Elias It looks like it could hold several hundred people easy.

Echo I'm not good at estimating things like that. At night I sit here and sometimes I can hear the past. I can hear what was here before now, who was here and what they were doing, laughing or yelling it's hard to make out the exact words like when you can hear someone in the room next door through a wall and it doesn't last long. Usually by the time I hear something it's already fading out again into the past. Like an echo. Yesterday I heard chickens scratching in the dirt.

Elias   My best guess is this was once a church. Or a market, or maybe a market first and then a church, or the other way around, or a church and then a cafeteria. People gathered here, in large numbers. They gathered and they did something together. For some reason El Patron wants to see The Orphan in person. Of all the thousands of properties he owns he decides to visit this place which just happens to be one I've lied to him about. Do you keep secrets?

Echo   I guess. Doesn't everybody?

Elias   I don't know. I lack empathy. I can't imagine anyone other than myself.

Echo   This clown told me once that secrets were what kept him warm. We'd be out somewhere with no heat in the wintertime and he'd be wearing a tee shirt and flip-flops. I'd ask him how he could stand it without a coat and he'd say to me, "I'm just burning my secrets. Long as I got my secrets I can't freeze to death."

Elias   The circus, for example. What a world that must be. I can't picture it. It's outside of my experience. I can't imagine how someone like you could have learned how to fly through the air.

Echo   It didn't take me long. The somersaults were easy, anyone can do that. The trick is knowing when to stop. When to reach out and grab the bar. My first month I caught a triple just like that, bang. Did it twenty-three nights in a row, then I lost it. Never caught one again. That's how it works, it's like a light switch. There's no 'almost' doing a triple. And once you lose it you better not press your luck. So I ran away. Most people run away to the circus. I ran away *from*. (*Pause.*) It wasn't long before I noticed other things happening to my body. There was a translation problem. I'd think turn left and my feet would turn right. It was as if my body started to have a mind of its own. I went to a doctor who said my body was producing too much electricity.

Elias	Is that serious?
Echo	One night I was out walking and garage doors lurched open as I passed by. Vending machines drop snacks if I get too close. That part is fun. I probably shouldn't have told you all that.

(*A man appears. It's* EL PATRON.)

El Patron	It's perfect.
Elias	I was just getting ready to send the report.
El Patron	No need for that now. (*He inhales deeply.*) The smell in here.
Elias	Mold.
El Patron	You say it like it's a bad thing. Don't believe the hype. Mold is fine. Jamón iberico. Life itself. Welcome to the Orpheum, young lady.
Elias	She used to be in the circus.
El Patron	Perfect. Everything has been liquidated. Except this. This is all I've got left.

Elias	It's a teardown for sure.
El Patron	What could be more ideal than an empty cavern, walls dripping with decay, floorboards rotting, windows boarded up. The perfect canvas for a thousand harebrained schemes.
Echo	I told him already. I don't know anything about this place.
El Patron	I need some people. A person. I'm looking for someone.
Echo	I can't help you.
El Patron	I had a hundred men working for me. I had ten trucks rolling round the clock. Then I took a fall. A bad fall. Shattered both elbows, the bones crushed to dust. I couldn't work. I needed help to squeeze toothpaste out of the tube. A coffee cup was impossible.
Echo	I've fallen. Far. I guess "falling" is more like it—because I don't know what the bottom is. Or 'where' the bottom is.
El Patron	I wouldn't need much. Some small movements, gestures, facial expressions. Showing your smile, hiding your smile. Baring your teeth. Not a lot in the way of props. Or lighting.
Echo	No audience.
El Patron	Maybe a few people. Maybe just one person.
Echo	I could do that.
El Patron	The marquesa reseats herself and raises her thin white hands. History throws light across the water. Civil liberties are lost. The sunset draws him to the rim. As dark clouds mantle the desert the directors of the looted railroad make a quick, undignified getaway. (*To* ELIAS.) Pack it up, son. We're outta here. (*To* ECHO.)

We'll be back.

(*El Patron exits. Elias follows.*)

El Patron (*As he goes.*) Nothing is better than nothing.

(*Echo watches them leave, then notices the audience. She slowly takes in the people, acknowledging their presence.*)

Echo Waiting is the loneliest of things, waiting for the one, the two, for the answer and the question both, finally, waiting for a signal, smoke on the horizon or just a ringtone, waiting to be picked up, waiting to be noticed without trying to be noticed, listening for the sound that will announce the waiting is over, or postponed, put off for another day, waiting for the next thing, the only thing that can possibly change waiting into something else, maybe hoping, maybe not.

The End

Giant Hollow Tooth

by Wesley Walker

Giant Hollow Tooth *was presented by Sharon's Farm at the Folly Bowl, July 2009, under the direction of Wesley Walker with the following cast:*

MOTHER	*Lisa Littman*
RANDY	*Andrew Hopper*
CAPTAIN ROMERO	*Gill Gayle*

Characters

MOTHER
RANDY
CAPTAIN ROMERO

Setting

A humble room in a military outpost near the equator.

(*A humble room in a military outpost near the equator. RANDY, an architect, is there with his MOTHER. RANDY has a blueprint spread out on the floor and makes edits with a pencil. He doesn't appear to know what he is doing.*)

Mother   I do like the landscape here, within The Compound. They keep it green. I like the trees that line the pond. It's poisonous, the pond—you've avoided it, I hope—but the garden, so reaching, so green, as if animated by some... mossy... will. I really do, I like it, Randy: it chimes with some wildness in me. Everything else about this place, though, makes me sick. The walls. The toilets. And, beyond The Compound...

Randy   Stop. Stop calling it The Compound, Mother. It's... they call it the "Garden Fort".

Mother   No it's luscious, the garden, a luscious exception to the arid, unhappy... It touches me. Pampas. Jonquils white, heliotrope. But the desert beyond... hope just cooks out there, human hope... you can feel it.

Randy   I'm nearly finished with my project plan, Mother. The Captain will be down soon to see it.

Mother   Let's hope he possesses a subtler mind than I.

Randy   Phases one and two, he's already approved them.

Mother   Let's hope he has a mind for subtlety, a mind which can contain air.

(*Pause.*)

Randy   I won't defend my designs to you. (*Pause.*) Why don't you put on a better blouse? Or improve your face somehow? We strive to impress the Captain.

Mother	Your father appeared substantial enough but his ideas were thin as air. What fundamental thing must a man be missing to produce ideas so paltry?
Randy	He was a dentist, mother.
Mother	A professor, a professor of dentistry.

(*Beats.*)

I just hope his son's ideas are... weightier. These people down here, Randy, they... they're rugged. You haven't overestimated their interest, I hope.

Randy	They've never seen a plan like this, Mother.
Mother	I hope you're right. I've sold the house.
Randy	You've sold our house?
Mother	Money—I don't know if you're aware, Randy—it's changed recently, it's...

(*Strange sound of clarinet in distance.*)

What's that sound?

Randy	It's the cry of the alpaca. The Captain approaches!

(*Fanfare, music off.*)

Mother	Money, Randy, has changed, it's...

(*Beats.*)

What binds us now is love.

(*They look at each other.* CAPTAIN ROMERO *enters. He carries a basket of fruit.*)

Captain	As your captain, I command you: enjoy. We have many vegetables. Some taste like blood. It's not everyday I meet a woman. When I do, I say, yes, history was bad to you: the bearer of our race, the basket of blood. And many hours of work. I am the Captain. Voices give way leaving only mine. Who will build the greatest shopping structure?

(*No response.*)

I will build the greatest shopping structure. There will be fountains and convenience. And one large eatery. Flan, someone will sell flan. Your son is crafty. How famous will he be? In many store windows you'll find a picture of me. In the picture I smile. Do I please the eye? Does nature, do earthquakes please the eye? We'll sell jackfruit, squash and lentil. We'll sell pelts of delicate fur. Do you demand that I submit to the world economy? I fart, a great wind is created, homes are lost. Your son is magic to me with his pencils. I receive deep pleasure. I contracted syphilis from a girl just like you. She wore her hair like a German. I taught her how to dance. Down here we've reduced gesture to essence. I point my penis, the woman delivers a child. It's not yet night, but the drinking mood pursues us. Wine, Randy! Wine! Let's all of us imbibe!

Mother	I am taken, Captain, quite more than taken, with your garden.
Captain	Yes.
Mother	It seems to contain an answer.

Captain	I point the penis, women spasm. We have wishes, doubts, but life hurls us into a tunnel. A wooden ball, hurled down a twisting chute or tunnel: not a single choice is mine. Only in retrospect can I see my choices. How tragic we are!! And yet look how I move my fingers! Look how I perfect the walk. You gave me syphilis, this was long ago. Over daiquiris. There's not a night since I haven't cried. You gave me a baby doll made of hair. When can we be alone together, when can we share our thoughts? I notice you are wounded.
Mother	No, I...
Captain	Let me see.
Mother	I don't think I...
Captain	Come. Come.

(*He pulls out a knife and cuts her hand. Red ribbons dangle from it.*)

Mother	Goodness! You've cut me!
Captain	Yes. Because humankind is full, too full.
Randy	Captain, I'm flattered you've approved of my plans.
Captain	Your son, lady! It's magic. His fingers! His pencils!
Randy	I've marshaled, for your sake, what usually constitutes the drab—the parking lot, the fire escapes—into a sort of material froth. I've felt my way, with your generous encouragement, to the very edge of form and, closing my eyes, leapt over.
Mother	I'm cut, bleeding.
Captain	Some of us have that problem. (*Captain cuts his own hand, red ribbons issue forth.*) Agh! Some of us share

	that problem. But you are a puzzle to me with your eyebrows and your grasp of history.
Mother	I... I have no grasp of...
Captain	(*As if quickly catching her up on the history.*) There was a war, a series of wars. I became captain. Then you opened your face.
Randy	People will shop, Captain, in your incomparable mall 'til they are nauseous. Goods, clothing will swarm at them like hornets. Every mirror, every surface...
Captain	Oh, oh, I hear the laughing! Who needs a mall in the desert? Where will the peasants find money to buy? But I love your son. He looks like me. And his ideas have terrible, terrible spikes. This is painful, this cut. I hope it goes away. But what is hope?
Mother	Randy. Will you find me a towel?
Randy	Priceless underwear, tools, cameras. In the food court you'll hear sobbing. The memory of a people drained... drained away...
Captain	I'm uncertain of my way, yet I barrel through, dragging with me men, children. I'm... I'm lost! But that doesn't stop me!
Randy	Men, grown men will throw themselves on shoppers to rape them. Teeth will be extracted. Everything, every single thing will hurt.
Captain	How I enjoy you, son! Once we've finished these drinks, I'd like us to step out to the veranda. But still I'm full. It's my own face that haunts me, grins at me teasingly from each object beheld. Perhaps another... (*Cuts himself again. More ribbons.*) Aggh! Better, better, yes, I think... aggh! Yes, your face opened like a hollyhock or the

vagina of a child. My stamen... I placed my stamen onto it. That's when time began. What will... What will life be like when I'm gone? Randy! What is wrong with your face?

Randy   I suppose it... it's registering concern, sir. For your sake. And... and loss.

Captain   The one dance I like best is the *Fortunato*. (*To* MOTHER.) Let me show you, darling. Come here.

(*He cuts her again. Ribbons.*)

Mother   Aggh!

Captain   We shrink! We shrink together. We're children.

Mother   Am I...? Am I in trouble? (*Beats.*) The jonquils, the harping bugs... respond. To a question I asked. (*Beats.*) A long time ago I asked them a question. And now they... (*Beats.*) Can you feel that?

Captain   Feel what, my dear?

Mother   Time?

(*They both age and expire as if in timed-exposure. RANDY ages too, exits. Music. RANDY, many years older now, returns. Since his last visit, a towering white mall of his design has been constructed. It's now boarded up, deserted.*)

Randy   Regret is too easy. Regret, remorse: they fool you into thinking you're paying down a debt. (*Beats.*) Yes, here it is: the shopping center we built. Constructed entirely of porcelain. Closed now, in many ways, many measurable ways, it was a success. Porcelain: to remind us of the human tooth. And to reflect back what's harshest of the sun. For the sun is harsh, growing harsher. Bullying its way into our lives. Hoping for… for what? Revelation? (*Beats.*) We refuse to regret what we did for progress.

(MOTHER *sits up, looks at* RANDY.)

Pain is but a doorway. Forget this, and you'll never be rich.

(*He turns his head, almost unbearably slowly, to look at* MOTHER. *They stare at each other. She blinks. She looks away. He waits. He looks away.*)

So unspeakably grand! The opportunities that await you!

(*The* CAPTAIN *sits up. He stares out vaguely.*)

Regret is for cowards. Shoulder the weight, the full weight of your offenses. Tremble. Tremble beneath it. You, my conspirators.

(*Slowly, slowly,* RANDY *diminishes in size. He is now the size of a plaything, a doll. The dead stare off. Music.*)

The End

Sabine River

by Sissy Boyd

Sabine River *was produced by Gunfighter Nation at Odyssey theater as part of* The Alamo Project, *Los Angeles, 2010, under the direction of John Steppling, with the following cast:*

BOATMAN   *Mark Rolston*
MOTHER   *Lisa Denke Littman*

Characters

BOATMAN
MOTHER

Setting

A rowboat with oars cocked, pulled up on a deserted beach.

Scene 1

(MOTHER moves along with BOATMAN's descriptions.)

Boatman I first saw her on the beach where I keep my boat. I ferry people to and from the island about an hour's ride away. She swept to the ocean's edge and stood staring at the water. I was not far from her. I felt she knew I was watching her. She gathered her skirts up and stepped sideways and stepped again and slapped her feet on the water. Step, slap, step, slap. She dropped her skirts and gathered them again. The daylight was fading. She walked toward me. She asked, is your boat in use? I answered, yes.

Mother I may bring my children tomorrow. They would enjoy a ride.

Boatman If the gloom lifts.

Mother Even then.

Boatman And she turned back to the water. I followed her. I asked, where are they now?

Mother With their Aunt Margaret.

Boatman She started to slap her feet on the water again. From side to side. Step, slap, turn. Step, slap turn. She bent over and cupped water and ran it through her hair. Then, more vehemently she slapped the water with her hands. She waded further in, turning and slapping. She turned to come out and wrung her skirts.

Mother Another warm evening. Do you live nearby? It must be very pleasant to live so close to the water.

Boatman Shall I see you tomorrow? With your children?

Mother	I'd like that. I'd like to know the names of the birds here.
Boatman	You're not from here? I asked her where she had slept.
Mother	I never sleep.
Boatman	Where are your children?
Mother	Soon.
Boatman	We waited.
Mother	They will come.
Boatman	Her eyes were turned to the dunes.
Woman	Here they come, now. (*Her eyes move from upstage to the boat, slowly. No children.*) Sabina and Little Brother. She never lets go of his hand. Children, climb into the boat.

*

Scene 2

(*Again,* MOTHER *moves to descriptions.*)

Boatman	I followed her down the beach, between the sea wall and the water. Where the sand was narrow she careened and stumbled in the tall grass. Where it was wide she stiffened. The wide space kept her fighting to stand. And on the narrow pathway she let herself go.
Mother	How old is she? Did she turn when you called?
Boatman	She froze. She's old.
Mother	You wanted to see her face.
Boatman	Yes, and I wanted to see her turn.
Mother	And did she?

Boatman	Slightly.
Mother	Was it beautiful?
Boatman	She's old. She was trembling. But yes.
Boatman	Her children are dead.
Mother	She said she didn't love them enough. Do you think that's true?
Boatman	There are stories. She tried to lose them when they were little. In a taxi, at an amusement park, in the ocean more than once. She tried to leave them in a taxi in the city. And at a theme park, but they clung to a guard until they saw her. As they grew she took them along. The daughter was beautiful, the brother was sweet. They were graceful. (*Pause.*) I hear.
Mother	She wasn't wretched?
Boatman	No. They swept along. She seemed serene.
Mother	But the children are dead. Dead?
Boatman	It may be that she was relieved.
Mother	She's old. Her beauty's gone. She never cared.
Boatman	There's no proof of anything. A boat and some blankets. Did she drown them? Some people say they drowned themselves to protect their mother. I saw them all once stopped in a clump. The children were staring at the back of her head. Would she turn and look at them, something? Didn't love them enough? They were all more and more inseparable. It can be a horror, what happens to children.
Mother	What did she think of herself? Why couldn't she let things be, send them away. To their father. She wasn't insane, not at all. She was bound to them, but not in the

way you think you know. I remember, she tried to lose them. She was waiting. But she wasn't insane.

Boatman The boatman was questioned. He remembers their agility. The mother asked,

Mother Is this the Sabine River? A beautiful name. My daughter's name is Sabina. And this is my son.

The End

A Dead Horse Beaten

by Marc Jensen

An earlier version of A Dead Horse Beaten *was presented in a workshop reading by Gunfighter Nation at The Lost Studio in Los Angeles, 2011, under the direction of the playwright with the following cast:*

TÓMAS   *Gray Palmer*
CAMILLE   *Heidi Darchuk*
EDGAR   *Michael Shamus Wiles*
ANDERSON   *Wesley Walker*

Characters

TÓMAS	*A man, supervisor of interrogation.*
CAMILLE	*A woman, subject of interrogation.*
EDGAR	CAMILLE's *husband.*
ANDERSON	*Subordinate to* EDGAR.

Setting

A black site.

Scene One

(Darkness. Lights up on TÓMAS, *forties, setting up a video camera on a tripod. He sits on a chair in front of the camera and pulls a ski mask on. With a remote, he signals the camera to begin filming. He sorts through a manila folder with various documents contained inside.)*

Tómas *(Clears throat, clears nostrils, exhales)* Mainsail off the starboard side. Wind blowing broad reaching... three knots. *(Pause.)* Sunup in approximately *(Looks at watch)* seventeen minutes. *(Pause)* GPS down... but by my calculations... our position is forty nautical miles from the northern most... "atoll" of the Marshall Islands *(Looks at map)*... Bokak. *(Pause. He sips on a cup of coffee and then continues.)*

The male detainee... conditions normal and consistent with age and effects of trauma... no major side effects to report from the anesthesia... some vomiting at first but that subsided after approximately two hours. Blood pressure down slightly... as to be expected. The EKG did detect an abnormality... but in checking the medical records, it's consistent with the diagnosis of a mild cardiac arrhythmia first detected in... *(Looks at chart.)* 1988... Bethesda. *(He casually tosses the chart aside.)*

No vitals to be recorded for the female detainee... none necessary. *(He leans back in his chair, away from the camera, sips the coffee.)*

The Overseer will be pleased to know the extraction is going... swimmingly.

(*Black out.*)

*

Scene Two

(*The sounds of the ocean, gentle rolling waves deep at sea. Spot from above up on a man,* EDGAR, *and a woman,* CAMILLE, *sitting on the floor, back to back, bound together with a thick rope.*)

Camille   We headed north... looking for the poor parts of whatever town we could find... West Memphis... North Little Rock... the Kentucky side of Cincinnati. (*Pause.*) Spent a good stretch on the Gulf Coast... Baton Rouge... Mobile... nothing suited us.

(*She leans back and rests her head on his shoulder.*)

We drove around the suburban parts of Shreveport... stopped at a Waffle House. We didn't eat... we just sat and listened. It was a foreign language ... "*hash browns—heavy*"... "*side of grits*"... "*Bs and Gs.*" The longer we sat there... listening... not ordering anything... the less anyone said... until the only sound was the

cook's spatula... *chink... chink... chink...* on the grill.
And everyone was watching... us.

(*Long pause. Sounds of loud waves crashing. The heads
of* CAMILLE *and* EDGAR *move in synchronization, rocking
back and forth with sound of the waves. She lifts her
head up again and resumes.*)

By the time we arrived in Bogotá—

Edgar   Bogotá?

Camille   Yes, Bogotá.

Edgar   I don't want to talk about Bogotá.

(*Pause.*)

Camille   So you... remember?

(*Black out.*)

*

Scene Three

(*Lights up on* CAMILLE *and* EDGAR, *bound back to back,
as before.*)

Camille   Every Thursday night, the general would invite us to his
           compound. Military brass... lots of Brits... oil

contractors... everyone to know in Riyadh would be there... drinking that home-brewed concoction of his. Tasted like vodka... with a shot of gasoline. (*Laughs.*) I still have the Polaroids from those parties.

(*She waits for a reaction from* EDGAR, *but there is none. They sit in silence.*)

Edgar So... I've been thinking... (*Pause.*) Ever seen what dehydration does to a person? (*Pause.*) By my calculations, we've got another 48 hours... before it really kicks in. (*Pause.*) I don't blame you... you know that, right? I really don't. (*Pause.*) I just hope that you don't blame me.

(*Black out.*)

*

Scene Four

(*Lights up.* CAMILLE *and* EDGAR *are tied together as before, looking more weary than before.* EDGAR *begins to clear his throat repeatedly as if he's trying to dislodge something. He pauses, then resumes clearing his throat.*)

Camille Please.

(EDGAR *stops clearing his throat.*)

| Edgar | Excuse me if my dying bothers you. |

(*Sound of a crashing wave.* CAMILLE *and* EDGAR *sway violently for a moment then stabilize.*)

Jesus, this fucking idiot doesn't know the first thing about sailing... has no clue what kind of a vessel he has in his hands. (*Pause.*) Don't say it.

Camille	Say what?
Edgar	Waste of money.
Camille	What are you talking about?
Edgar	I'll show you a waste of money. (*Pause.*) I work you know.

(*Long pause.* EDGAR *tries to hold back but he cannot and resumes clearing his throat.* CAMILLE *hangs her head.*)

(*Black out.*)

*

Scene Five

(*Lights up. They are tied as before.* CAMILLE *begins to speak, but stops, mid-thought. They sit for a moment. She licks her lips, begins to turn her head toward* EDGAR *to speak, but again stops herself.*)

(*Black out.*)

Scene Six

(*Lights up. Same scene. Edgar is asleep. Camille tries to carefully turn around and look at the Edgar, but is unable to do so. She looks up at the ceiling.*)

Camille (*Whispers.*) Tómas... (*She waits. Nothing. Whispers.*) Tómas... (*She waits. Nothing.*) Goddamnit... the prompter went out. (*She waits. Nothing.*) Tómas?

(*Black out.*)

Scene Seven

(*Lights up. Tómas stands over Camille with another manila folder filled with documents. Edgar is unconscious and appears bloodied and beaten.*)

Tómas I reviewed your files again... and according to your tax returns... your last good year together was '95. You made 180 grand the two of you... had a nice home in El Paso... good friends... lifelong friends... the kind you could go on Alaskan cruises with when you got up in your years. (*Pause.*) But as good as it was there... something still wasn't right, was it? You didn't belong there with your money. El Paso... it's not a place you just move to and make a living. (*Pause.*) Ever think about having children?

(CAMILLE *spits at* TÓMAS.)

I have no problem killing him, you know.

Camille He doesn't remember a goddamn thing, OK?

Tómas If it's the money you're concerned about, the Overseer rewards cooperation... quite handsomely I might add. (*Clears his throat.*) As I was saying... ever think about having children Camille? (*Long pause.*)

Camille There wasn't time.

Tómas Don't you think it would have been beneficial if you'd had something tangible to point to after all these years?

Camille The time... it was never right.

(EDGAR *moans.*)

Tómas You know, Camille, some mornings, I wake up and I'll notice something tangible... like, say, a blood stain on the Berber and even though I'm not happy about it... that stain... it shows me something... it shows me that I've done something with my life.

Camille I... I'll keep trying.

(*TÓMAS stands over her, contemplating. After a moment, he pulls out a canteen and puts it to her lips. She drinks.*)

Tómas   You know what gets me Camille? Still to this day... I can't fathom how a seemingly "regular guy"... can visit a foreign land and just walk up to a man like that... a dignitary for God's sake... and... blow his fucking brains out... and then just walk away like he's... walking out of a movie or something... and then poof... just vanish... back into the grid.

(*Black out.*)

*

Scene Eight

(*Lights up on EDGAR and CAMILLE as before. EDGAR is conscious, albeit with black eyes, bruises and smeared blood on his face.*)

Camille   Walter Reed?

Edgar   (*Straining to speak.*) I remember that male nurse... the one with the lazy eye... he was poisoning me.

Camille   The leg braces... they gave you an infection.

Edgar   I told him the codes and the coordinates but he didn't write anything down... he just stared at me with that fucking eye.

Camille	You were on a lot of meds.

(*Long pause.*)

Edgar	You fucked him, didn't you?
Camille	Oh Jesus...
Edgar	You did. I saw you with my own eyes sucking his lazy cock...sucking it right off. (*Pause.*) I wasn't as unconscious as it may have looked.
Camille	You're delusional.
Edgar	No, I'm thirsty. (*Pause.*) Delusional. (*Pause.*) I've never been more lucid in my entire life.

(*Black out.*)

*

Scene Nine

(TÓMAS, *ski mask on, stands before* CAMILLE. EDGAR *is unconscious.*)

Tómas	Again.
Camille	I'm tired.
Tómas	Again.
Camille	He's on to us...
Tómas	He's bluffing.

(TÓMAS walks over to EDGAR and taps him with his foot.)

Tómas   He doesn't know what he knows and what he doesn't know.

Camille   He's going to wake up—

Tómas   He won't be waking up anytime soon. Not after the beating I just administered. *(Pause.)* Again.

Camille   I've got it down.

Tómas   I don't think you've got it at all. You've only got another 24 hours before... he's dead and we're out of business. We'll do this again and again and again until it's pitch perfect. *(Long pause.)* Now compose yourself... and let's pick it up from Log page 487.4... the right hand column... '92... March.

Camille   *(Listlessly.)* Jackson... we bought a Craftsman... a three-two... two and a half actually... in the historic part of town. You wanted something—

Tómas   Jackson? Tennessee?

Camille   Yes.

Tómas   No, not plausible. Nashville... Memphis... maybe Knoxville. But Jackson? No, not you. Again.

Camille   *(Sighs.)* You always liked Tahoe so we decided to try Reno out for a stretch... we lived at the Golden Nugget for several weeks... to get our bearings. Had the Presidential suite... money was no object. You always liked roulette and the novelty of getting breakfast any time of day...

Tómas   Good... good... keep going.

(Black out.)

*

Scene Ten

> *(Lights up on EDGAR. CAMILLE is asleep. EDGAR yells out loud.)*

Edgar I'm a consultant… a private consultant. (*He looks up at the spot above. But there is no reaction.*) Fuck you… I don't care if you believe me. I know people who could fucking wipe you off the grid. (*Long pause. He continues.*) This is the most amateur operation I've ever been a part of, you hear me? Amateur. You want my confession? Well here it is motherfucker. Last job I did was for a company that made blinds. Fucking blinds for windows! The whole supply chain in their pocket… but they couldn't make up the margins… couldn't charge enough… people will only pay a certain amount for shitty metallic blinds… even if they are custom. I turned it around from a four-day turnaround to a three-day. Margins are higher. Customers are happier. Windows have their blinds a whole day earlier.
One fucking day!
Is that what you want?
I work for a living motherfucker!

> *(Black out.)*

Scene Eleven

(TÓMAS sets up the video camera on the tripod as before. He sits in the chair, manila folder in hand, and prompts the camera with the remote. He places an earbud in his ear.)

Tómas   Our position is approximately eight nautical miles from the southern coast of Tahiti... just a day... or so... behind schedule. *(TÓMAS listens to the headset.)* Yessir, I know. I think we're close. I think he's ready to... reconcile his position. *(TÓMAS listens again.)* She's cooperating... some. *(He squirms in his chair.)* But sir, I have confidence that—*(He listens intently and adjusts himself in the chair.)* Today? *(He listens more and is subdued.)* I'll prepare the cabin for his arrival.

(Black out.)

*

Scene Twelve

(Lights up on CAMILLE tied up as before, but in the place EDGAR, she's bound to a mannequin.)

| Camille | I was so sure that time in Atlanta. Could really feel it. (*Pause.*) We walked around the Coca Cola headquarters. I remember everyone looking at me... so curious... the gazes. It wasn't until I felt the drops of blood on my ankles that I realized why. (*Laughs.*) That was the closest we ever came. Probably for the best, huh? (*Pause.*) You know, the other day, when you were on one of your trips... I was feeling sorry for myself. I was. I paced every inch of the house... just looking at our things. Even went into the pantry. Did you know we have beef bouillon cubes that have been with us for twenty years? I actually started to cry. Can you believe it? (*Laughs.*) And then I found myself in my closet... looking at all of the clothes ... beautiful suits I never wear... scarves... pashminas. I dressed myself up... like we were going to a state department dinner or some other god-awful affair. (*Laughs.*) Oh Edgar... when I think about it, really stop to think about it... we've got it good. (*She leans back touching her head to the back of the mannequin's. She senses the difference in feel. She sits up.*) (*Black out. In the darkness, a gunshot rings out. After a moment, another gunshot rings out.*) |

*

Scene Thirteen

(*Lights up slowly on* EDGAR *sitting at a large desk, shirt off. Another* MAN *stands behind him, massaging his shoulders while* EDGAR *looks through a stack of files. Behind them stands a row of large filing cabinets. After several moments,* EDGAR *motions for the* MAN *to stop. The* MAN *wipes the oil from* EDGAR'S *shoulders with a towel and waits.*)

Man   Would you prefer to be alone, sir?

Edgar   Stay... go... I don't give a shit.

(EDGAR *stands and buttons his shirt. He pours himself a drink, finishes it, then pours another.*)

Man   It couldn't be helped, sir. (*A long pause.*) You realize that it couldn't be helped.

Edgar   Shut up.

(EDGAR *finishes his drink and throws the glass against the wall, shattering it into pieces.*)

Edgar   Do you know who I am... what the fuck's your name again?

Man   Anderson, sir.

Edgar   Do you know what I'm capable of, Anderson?

(ANDERSON *shakes his head.*)

I once made a man eat his own excrement. I burned another man's foot with a blowtorch until he sold me his horse. Lost every toe on the right one, I'm sure of it. (*Pause.*) Do you know what that does to a man, Anderson? What it does to his marriage? To come home after a day like that and try to do things... normal things? Just try Anderson... just you try fucking your wife after a day like that.

Anderson   It won't happen again sir.

Edgar   The whole damn operation... the training... planning... all of it... fucked.

Anderson   Sir, I can assure you—

Edgar   Shut the fuck up Anderson. Just shut the fuck up before I cut your goddamn tongue out.

(*ANDERSON stands still momentarily before finally walking over and collecting the broken glass. He holds the pieces in his hands, unsure of where to dispose of them, before putting them in his pants pocket.*)

Edgar   Anderson.

Anderson   Sir?

Edgar   I want you to do something.

Anderson   Why of course, sir. (*Pause. ANDERSON waits for the order.*) Anything you say—

Edgar   I want you to burn all of this shit.

(*Long pause.*)

Anderson   Sir?

Edgar   The files... burn them all to hell.

(*ANDERSON doesn't move.*)

Goddamnit... why is it that no one listens to me? Why is it that I'm forced to shoot someone in the fucking face to get anyone to pay attention to me? Why? Why Anderson? Tell me why?

(ANDERSON *reluctantly walks over to one of the file cabinets. He opens the drawer and pulls out a manila folder and empties its contents on the ground. He repeats the process folder after folder until the ground is covered with papers.*)

(*Black out.*)

The End

Those Who Get Close

by Christopher Kelley

Those Who Get Close *was presented by Sharon's Farm, Folly Bowl, 2011. It was directed by the playwright with the following cast:*

BILL   *Hank Bunker*
STACY   *Jacqueline Wright*

Characters

BILL   *A man in ragged carpenter's pants and no shoes.*
STACY   *A woman in a cocktail dress.*

Setting

A field at dusk.

(BILL stands downstage in ragged carpenter's pants and no shoes. He looks very sick. STACY is far stage right in a cocktail dress with a glass of wine. BILL doesn't see her.)

Bill   The Baptists use snakes to envision their saints. But I do believe the widow is holier.

As a boy, I held a horse around the neck and listened to the blood in her. It was the sound of the truth of love. She had lost her colt and the blood in her veins sang of her grief. I could hear those kinds of things when I was a boy.

But I couldn't hold on.

These days I have a kind of sanctuary in a barn which is full of widows. When you're very still and very quiet, they come close in numbers. Once bitten I faced death, it's true, but bitten repeatedly and constantly, I've come to endure.

The venom puts the spider in your blood. Dreams of thoraxes and carapaces and a thousand spinnerets bedevil you awake or asleep. And I am always awake. Each dusk as the darkness comes on, I cascade into the underworld of the arachnid but not to sleep and I am soon beset by the legs and mandibles of countless fever bringing beasties all fanging me and pumping god knows how much horror into my veins.

Hopped up on black poison, one sees with many eyes. It may be my mind, but I like to think not.

And I wonder if you see me.

I never step off the bed because that would mean going on the floor in bare feet where a multitude of scorpions war each night. But I dare not put my boots on because the damp warmth of a person's shoes attracts the blood scarab whose jaws can sever an artery like iron shears.

There are many reasons not to leave that bed, teeming though it is. But anymore, I confess I find the widow's flavor of poison desirable above all others. It is, in its gruesome way, holy on those nights when the visions transport me back to my youth and I see what might have been; what almost was. I hold on to those. I hold on as long as I can. Listening to the truth of love.

Stacy I can hear what you're thinking. I hear every word Bill and you're wrong. So wrong. The truth of love is, if you're lucky, it destroys absolutely and you don't have to do it yourself. But you're out ahead of me there. (*Pause.*) And dinner's ready.

Bill Oh. Hello Stacy. I'm not hungry dear. I am just not in an eating mood. But thank you. Thanks.

Stacy It's not healthy to be all alone. Not all the time. You start talking to yourself… imagining things. Replaying the past which, honestly, I am certain is best left not reviewed. Because it always causes one to see shit that's never really there.

Bill I wish you wouldn't overhear me.

Stacy Who listens? You're alone, bleating at empty heaven for all the world like a thousand liars. It troubles me, Bill.

I'm troubled. Do you even see how dark it's getting?
While you're starving yourself and babbling at holes in
the sky. I can scarcely see you out here. You've withered
away to virtually nothing and so, you see, this is the
trouble. This is how come I am troubled. Unlike
yourself, I don't want to disappear. (*Long pause.*) And
what the fuck are you doing out in the neighbor's barn
all night? Would you like to talk about that? What are
you waiting for out there.

Bill   I just don't like to hear my voice anymore Stacy. It's quiet
out there.

Stacy   Quiet? Because I can year you howling all the way down
in the TV room.

Bill   You shouldn't listen.

Stacy   Several gay men have befriended me Bill. Did you know
that? Gay men from that big church over the lake. They
pity me. How does that sound? And why is that? And
what do you talk about out there?

Bill   I go to the barn to sleep.

Stacy   Who could sleep in that horrible place? I've seen it; it's
crawling with shit I don't want to know about.

Bill   Then don't ask.

Stacy   Maybe I enjoy lies anymore. Maybe I have become
accustomed to them.

You're waiting for someone. Isn't that so? Lost men
waiting for someone in a dark place. I'm not jealous. Just
really troubled. Maybe it's a woman, maybe it's someone
else. Some imaginary savior. You see why this troubles
me? What you're waiting for, Bill? You see why that

	mystery would trouble a girl who's accustomed to lies. And how that might make you think, make one think that I want to try to kind of destroy you... As a favor.
Bill	I sleep the sleep of Joseph out there.
Stacy	And how did he die?
Bill	What?
Stacy	I asked: How did Joseph die?
Bill	He was martyred. He died Stacy. Shit, I don't know.
Stacy	Because I doubt he slept for shit after they killed his son.

(*Bill stares at her. Long pause.*)

	You don't sleep, Billy. You don't even close your fucking eyes for fear of who might appear.
Bill	I suspect he held on. Tried to sort it all out and I imagine he did his best. They made him a saint but who knows. He did his work and held on and I don't think she asked much more of him. Not much at all, I'd guess, once their boy went to the cross.
Stacy	Did he move her out to some desolate wasteland? Did they abandon all comfort for the country?
	You suppose he lied to her to protect her?
Bill	What?
Stacy	You think Joe told Mary a sack of lies to protect her?

(*Pause. He turns to go.*)

How about that mare, Billy? The one who threw the dead colt? And your mother's agony. The mare and the sickly colt? The scars on your father's hands. The iron shear and the hollow sound of the tanner's axe. Come in and tell me about the horse, Bill.

Who loved that mare after her colt went off to the glue factory?

Bill	I suppose he held on. Maybe he had to fib here and there, regarding his notions mostly about the dead kid... Who knows, Stacy. How do I know what a saint does.
Stacy	She must have needed some comfort... who took her in his arms after that farrier hauled away her colt?
Bill	I looked after the mare.
Stacy	And you listened. You could still hear love though she was half dead.
Bill	She grieved so hard they shot her.

(*Long pause.*)

Stacy	Are you going back to the barn tonight?
Bill	God only fucking knows.
Stacy	But you're going back to the barn.
Bill	I don't have much choice.
Stacy	Have you looked at yourself? The next bite will do you.
Bill	I know that.
Stacy	Here's my guess. You stood up when they came for the mare. They had a bead on her and you stood up.
Bill	My father. "Get aside whelp, or I'll shoot you too."
Stacy	Yet here you are, poor little fellow.
Bill	I held on. Around her neck. And I told her that she would be alright. I told her she'd get through, that we all

	would and it would be better soon. That my love would heal her wound.
Stacy	But that was a lie.
Bill	Yes it was. We do that at those times whether we mean to or not.
Stacy	And here's the thing: she knew it before the kid died. Love doesn't heal when it comes to this. When it goes that way.

(*Long pause.*)

| **Bill** | I'm going to the barn now Stacy. |
| **Stacy** | There's a little hole in the middle of everyone's heart. You're born with it. Above the chamber where the blood flows in and out, there's this little nugget of emptiness without which, the valves would seize up. It's like a room for staying alive. Doctors don't have a name for it. They'll tell you it's a murmur. But they don't know. It's there. Deep in the center of the heart and no one can hear it but you. When that sound is gone, it means that little space has flooded; seized up and you're dead. |

(*He turns to her.*)

| **Bill** | They don't talk about Joseph after the kid died. All anyone wants to read is how Mary held a dead boy in her arms and how she ascended into heaven. But the stories about the father just end at carpentry. |

| Stacy | It destroys slowly like a million poisons or, at times, suddenly as a shot. A thousand cuts and floods. |

(*Long pause. BILL doesn't know which way to go.*)

| Bill | I'm going to the barn. |

(*He goes to exit but stops at the wings and listens with his back to her.*)

| Stacy | Look up there, Billy. He's coming down the hill now. You were wrong, like I told you a thousand times. He's not dead, Bill. What a fool you were to go out there and suffer alone with all those little demons. Look up over the hill there. You see him coming? You see that? What a boy he is. Look now, he's waving. Wave back Billy. Give our boy a reason to come on down that hill. |

(*BILL exits.*)

I don't need anything to see him. I don't need anything to see him.

The End

How to Talk to the Dead

by Chris Rossi

An earlier version of How to Talk to the Dead *was presented by Gunfighter Nation at The Lost Studio, Los Angeles, 2011, under the direction of the playwright with the following cast:*

SHANNA   *Meredith Bishop*
HOWARD   *Jan Munroe*
PATRICIA   *Cinda Jackson*

Characters

SHANNA	*Nineteen*
HOWARD	*Fifties*
PATRICIA	*Fifties*

Scene One

(*Howard's room.*)

Shanna   I don't know what to do.

Howard   Let me be the guide.

(*Howard points to a chair. Shanna sits. She holds herself. He sits opposite her. Silence.*)

Look at me.

(*She does.*)

Uncross your arms.

(*She does.*)

Relax.

(*She tries. They sit there. After a beat:*)

Shanna   The whole room is hot.

Howard   (*Nods.*) I've opened a channel.

(*Pause.*)

Shanna   My hands are on fire.

Howard   That's a normal response.

(*Pause.*)

Shanna   What's happening now?

Howard   I'm sensing a presence.

(*Pause.*)

Shanna   Here in this room?

Howard   Just entering our plane.

(*Pause.*)

Shanna   Where?

Howard   Not fully arrived...

Shanna   Can you see him?

Howard   (*Opens his eyes. Stares intensely at something.*) Yes.
(*Then.*) There you are.

Shanna   Where?

Howard   Behind you.

Shanna   Oh God.

Howard   Look at me.

Shanna   (*Trembling.*) I'm on fire.

Howard   Don't turn around.

(*Lights out.*)

*

Scene Two

(*HOWARD and SHANNA in chairs, facing each other.*)

Howard Where are you?

Shanna Walking along the shoreline. He was holding my hand. There were waves crashing at our legs... I was scared I would be swept out.

Howard But with his protection...

Shanna (*Nods.*) I was safe.

Howard Another?

Shanna (*Beat.*) There's a highway. Rush hour traffic. I'm... six years old. He wants me to cross. He's waiting on the other side. He tells me to wait until the light changes, but I can't. I don't want to be apart from him. So I step off the curb and start running... cars and trucks swerving not to hit me... my heart is racing... I make it to the middle... between the lanes. Where the grass is. The island. The verge. (*Pause*) I look across the other lanes... and my heart stops. I can't see him on the other side. He's not where he said he would be. He was hiding. Playing a trick on me. (*Pause*) And I thought, "no one will come and get me." "No one will take me across."

(*Silence.*)

Howard How did he pass?

Shanna He did it to himself.

(*Pause.*)

Howard	I will take you across. (*Off her look.*) We're going farther now. Deeper than before. To achieve an ultimate merging.
Shanna	How?
Howard	A sacred object will serve as a locus of connection.
Shanna	An object?
Howard	Something of great importance to him.
Shanna	He left nothing behind.
Howard	That's not exactly true.

(*Pause.*)

Shanna	Do you mean me? (*Off his look.*) I don't think I can. (*SHANNA, frustrated, holds herself.*)
Howard	(*Calm.*) There's a world we're all trying to... access. A world invisible to us but just... beyond our plane of understanding. A place where secrets and wisdom and... energy abide. God is there. And your father. And all our ancestors. But first we must build a bridge. To arrive in that place. And once we do, we find what we seek. All our answers wait for us. Do you understand?
Shanna	Yes.
Howard	Let me be the guide. (*Then.*) Uncross your arms.

(*She does.*)

Look at me.

(*She does. HOWARD extends his arms, palms up. He closes his eyes.*)

Repeat after me: The Channel is Light.

Shanna	"The Channel is Light."
Howard	The Light is a Door.
Shanna	"The Light is a Door."
Howard	And the Door now will open.
Shanna	The door will now...

(*HOWARD rises slowly, and stands behind her.*)

| Howard | ... Open. |
| Shanna | Open. |

(*HOWARD, places his hands on her shoulders. Strokes her hair. Closes his eyes. Lights out.*)

*

Scene Three

(*HOWARD and SHANNA. Shanna's arm hangs down, palm open. After a beat of silence—*)

Shanna	He's holding my hand.
Howard	We're making him welcome.
Shanna	Why does he come?
Howard	To give you his message.

Shanna	And what is his message?
Howard	He wants you at peace. Because... he is... at peace. (*Pause.*) And he wants you to know.... he never suffered.
Shanna	Is that what he says?
Howard	It's there in his eyes.
Shanna	There's nothing else?
Howard	What more could there be?
Shanna	(*Beat.*) Could you be wrong?
Howard	My method is flawless.
Shanna	But could you be wrong?
Howard	You're losing your focus.

(SHANNA *looks increasingly distraught.*)

Shanna	I don't know. It doesn't sound like him.
Howard	What?
Shanna	That... That he would say that. (*Suddenly rising.*) He wants something from me. He wants me to do something.
Howard	What?
Shanna	I don't know. Something. He won't tell me. (*Then.*) Why won't he tell me? Why won't you tell me?

(*They stare at each other. Lights out.*)

*

Scene Four

(HOWARD *and* SHANNA.)

Shanna   I don't think I can pay you any more.

Howard   We'll work something out.

Shanna   I've pretty much given you all I have.

Howard   But we've only begun.

Shanna   He hasn't spoken. He hasn't told me what he wants.

Howard   We'll keep the channel open.

Shanna   I don't have forever.

Howard   Ah, but you do. We all do.

Shanna   (*Pause.*) I feel like my life was a boat on the ocean and I fell off it. I'm trying to swim after it. My arms are getting tired. I don't think I'm going to make it.

Howard   (*Pause.*) I'm sure he was a good man.

(SHANNA *stares at him.*)

Shanna   You are? Why is that?

Howard   It is not for you to judge. We encounter many people throughout our lifetimes. But you never know which of your significants will have the most valence for you.

Shanna   "Valence"?

Howard   The power of attraction embodied in another person. (*Off her silence.*) This is your life. This moment. This place.

Shanna   "Here?" Like, this room?

Howard   Why not?

Shanna   Well, it's your life too.

*(*Howard *puts his hands on her.)*

I want to do what you do. I want to help people. Like you did on your TV show.

Howard	(*Looking away.*) You're helping me right now.
Shanna	I am?
Howard	Where are you living?
Shanna	(*Shrugs.*) I stay with different people.
Howard	Different men?
Shanna	(*She looks at him.*) You're funny.
Howard	(*Pause. He moves away.*) I'm going to give you a number. A special number, a private number for my other phone. You call it anytime you need something. Day or night. Okay? I'm also going to give you... a gift. The gift of a message. A message that will forever bond us.

*(*Howard *scribbles a number on the back of a business card. He stops. Then writes something else—a short message. He hands it to her. She reads it.)*

Shanna	Oh wow. This is...
Howard	You remember that.
Shanna	This is really...
Howard	Carry it in your heart.
Shanna	Where is it from?
Howard	A dream. From a very powerful voice I heard when I was deeply tuned in. I awoke and immediately wrote it down. It's one of the guiding forces of my life. And I give it to you.

Shanna	Wow. I owe you one.
Howard	You owe me nothing.
Shanna	That's not exactly true.

(*They look at each other. Silence. SHANNA begins unbuttoning her shirt.*)

| Howard | What? |

(*He just stands there. As SHANNA takes a step toward him and puts a hand on his chest.*)

| Shanna | I'm open to receive now. I really think this is going to be the one. |

(*Lights out.*)

*

Scene Five

(*HOWARD in bed. SHANNA standing in the center of the room.*)

| Howard | Come back. |
| Shanna | I have to be somewhere. |

(*Silence. They look at each other.*)

Howard	You spoke in your sleep.
Shanna	What did I say?
Howard	"I'm going to the bridge." (*Off her silence.*) What does that mean?
Shanna	(*Beat.*) You opened a channel. (*Pause.*) I've been given the message.
Howard	(*He looks at her, frustrated.*) It's only a dream.
Shanna	He comes to me now.
Howard	That's not how it works.
Shanna	No? How does it work?
Howard	(*Pause.*) Look at me.
Shanna	No.
Howard	(*He looks at her, desperate.*) The message comes through me. The message always comes through me. The message *must* come through me.

(*She stares at him, smiling.* LIGHTS OUT.)

*

Scene Six

(*Sounds of rush hour, freeway traffic.* SHANNA *walks across the stage. She wears a ragged, thrift store, man's winter coat.* SHANNA *stops, looks out. Lights out.*)

*

Scene Seven

(HOWARD *alone in his room. He strokes his chest, as* SHANNA's *voice plays over.*)

Shanna   (*Offstage*) There's a road. With traffic. Four lanes. I'm... six years old. He wants me to cross. He's waiting on the other side. He tells me to wait until the light changes, but I can't. I don't want to be apart from him. So I step off the curb and start running... cars and trucks going by me... my heart racing... I make it to the middle... between the lanes. Where the grass is. The island. The verge.

(*Black out.*)

*

Scene Eight

(HOWARD *and* PATRICIA. *Silence. She looks at him.*)

Patricia   Help me understand.
Howard   We know what we know.

(*Silence.*)

Patricia   There was a spider on the curtain in the house she grew up in. She wouldn't let the cat go near it. I watched her put it in a tissue and carry it outside and let it go on the driveway. Life was so precious to her.

Howard	These things don't go unnoticed.
Patricia	By whom?
Howard	Higher powers.
Patricia	(*Stares at him.*) I saw this... with her. All of it... I saw it coming.
Howard	Perhaps you have a gift.
Patricia	Oh, I have a gift, all right. (*Then.*) How could you?
Howard	Intimacies develop during the procedure. A bond forms. Once the channel opens.
Patricia	How did it start? Regular appointments? Like a "professional?"
Howard	She doesn't respond to boundaries.
Patricia	You're telling me what she was like?
Howard	I'm sorry for your loss.

(*Pause.* PATRICIA *takes a small, wrinkled business card out of her purse.*

(HOWARD *looks uneasy. Pause.*

Where did you get that?

Patricia	The Highway Patrol. (*Beat.*) It was tucked in her shoe. Or what was left of it. They found it on the other side of the divide.
Howard	I wanted to leave her with some wisdom.
Patricia	(*She holds up the card.*) You think this is wisdom?
Howard	It came from my dream.

(Silence. She just stares at him.)

Patricia   I know people. People I grew up with. They wouldn't hesitate to help me. You understand? Find you at a rest stop somewhere, in the trunk of a car. A hole blown through your face.

Howard   *(Pause.)* This isn't you.

Patricia   *(Beat.)* What? What isn't?

(He points to the chair.)

Howard   Sit down.

Patricia   No...

(He remains pointing. Until she sits.)

Howard   Relax.

Patricia   What isn't me?

Howard   I am the guide.

Patricia   *(Confused.)* What are we doing?

Howard   Look at me.

(She does. Silence. She starts to break down.)

(Calm.) There's a world we're all trying to... access. A world invisible to us but just... beyond our plane of understanding. A place where secrets and wisdom and... energy abide. God is there. And your daughter. And all

our ancestors. But first we must build a bridge. To arrive
in that place. And once we do, we find what we seek.
All is revealed. Do you understand?

(*A beat. She nods. Lights out.*)

*

Scene Nine

(HOWARD *sits in a chair. Listening as a recording of one
of his old shows plays.*)

Howard   (*Offstage.*) ...and I'm sensing a name. Something
beginning with the letter... I'm getting the letter "M."
Stand up please. Yes, you. There's a radiant spirit
around you. Can you feel it? Trust me. It's there.
And in that spirit I see a figure. Yes. I see... an older
man. (*Beat.*) He spent some time in hospital, at the end
of his life. A father figure. No? But a mentor, yes? An
uncle, perhaps? Yes. Of course. And you were close
when you were young. I know this to be true. (*Beat.*)
He's telling you something. It's very clear. Would you
like to know what it is? (*Beat.*) He wishes you peace.
He wants you to know how much he loved you in his
life. And he is so proud... so very proud... of what you
have become.

(Sudden applause from a studio audience. HOWARD holds himself. Closes his eyes. A pin light reveals SHANNA, standing behind him. Silence. HOWARD rises, trembling.)

Shanna Don't turn around.
(Black out.)

The End

Small Planet

by Sharon Yablon

Small Planet *was presented by Sharon's Farm on a street in Echo Park, Los Angeles, 2012, under the direction of the playwright with the following cast:*

KEN   *Adrian Alex Cruz*
MARA   *Jacqueline Wright*

Setting

Los Angeles, 1970s.

Author's Note

The audience should be small, and will follow the actors on a walk around the hills as they perform the play.

(KEN *and* MARA *stand on the street in a residential part of Echo Park.* KEN *holds a small, handmade doll.*)

Ken   It looks like a devil doll to me. You know, like something handmade.

Mara   Don't get me wrong. I'm not really afraid of it.

Ken   Why'd you call me then?

(*She takes it back from him.*)

Mara   Someone left it on my doorstep...

(*She is drawn in by the doll momentarily. The actors begin their walk.*)

Ken   Could be from a Vietnamese gang. You had any problems with them?

Mara   Just the usual.

Ken   Asian gangs can be pretty fierce. You might not think so, as they're a slight people. They don't really look like men, do they? With their lack of body hair. Smooth skin. It's as if those eyes are begging to be conquered.

(MARA *stops, smells something on* KEN *she doesn't like.*)

Mara   Is that patchouli oil?

Ken   I don't know.

Mara   Well are you wearing it or not?

Ken   Yeah, I always just put some on when I leave the house.

(Pause, she's irritated. She looks up at a small house behind her; they resume their walk.)

Mara   I don't know how long I should wait to get another roommate. When do you think a person should be considered dead?

Ken   If you never see the body... lots of people go missing. You go to Mexico, you'll find that. You leave a taqueria there and walk right into the ether.

Mara   If she was killed by the Hillside Strangler, she would be part of L.A. history, forever. That is kinda cool.

(They stop; she gestures to a nearby hillside.)

Mara   I was riding my bike past one of the hills where they had just found a body. The girl's eyes were open and there were black and blue hand marks around her neck, like this. *(Puts her hands on her neck, as if strangling.)* Her hair was parted down the middle, just like Marcia Brady.

Ken   That's what the killers like.

Mara   Her face was bloated but you could still tell she was pretty.

(He looks dreamily at her.)

Ken   You'd still be pretty if you were bloated too.

(They continue their walk.)

What could be better than starting a cult? There's a trendy vegetarian restaurant for sale; I'm going to buy it.

Mara You don't have any money.

Ken I'm going to turn it into my personal recruiting depot for freaky tantric experimentation.

(*She's nonplussed.*)

Now in case you think I'm just jonesin' for sex with underage teens, or that I'm starting an end of days cult—I realized this during insomnia—people in Los Angeles want love and sex! They want a home and a girlfriend they can share. My restaurant is on the Strip for a reason. It will be a beacon to homeless children! Lost rockers will come out of the hills! But. Isn't there some sort of celestial happening tonight?

Mara There's a comet party.

Ken Hmmm, I wasn't invited.

(*They both stop, look up at the sky.*)

It's like a white smear in the sky... my father is sick and we pretend to be worried but the truth is, we're all quietly waiting for him to die.

(*They start walking again.*)

Do you know that Sunset Boulevard is a very diverse street?

Mara I don't really care.

Ken It goes from East L.A., all through Hollywood and Beverly Hills. Through the Palisades, and then out to Malibu and the coast. Schwab's Pharmacy was there, where Lana Turner was discovered. Did you know that F. Scott Fitzgerald had a heart attack while buying a pack of cigarettes, right in the store? Charlie Chaplin used to play pinball in a back room. "Over the Rainbow" was written right across the street. Where that El Pollo Loco is, there used to be a hotel called the Garden of Allah.

(*She picks a flower.*)

I remember the noise that came out of my parent's room. It was a terrible sounding noise, but as I grew older it bothered me less.

(*They start walking again.*)

Did you hear about the building they demolished downtown? They found a flute glass in the dirt from the 1800s under it. And a piece of this beautiful red and gold wallpaper with fleur-de-lys. That's all that was left of what was obviously a bordello that probably serviced prospectors coming here during the Gold Rush.

Mara (*Stops.*) I have to go meet Jeremy now.

Ken Oh. I thought that.

Mara Look. I'm not going to fuck you. Okay?

Ken Oh, I know. It's just. You called me because you were scared of that devil doll.

Mara	I wasn't scared.
Ken	Well, do you think you should be wandering around with the Hillside Stranglers at large?
Mara	They're only killing in Glendale.
Ken	These aren't the first serial killers here. But it's the first team. (*Pause.*) Well, I guess you're okay for now.
Mara	I'm going to the comet party.

(*She walks away, disappearing around a corner.* KEN *is left alone.*)

Ken	Don't go to Glendale! (*Pause, he fidgets, looks up at the hills.*) I guess I'll go up to Griffith Park. They'll probably have the power telescopes out. (*Pause.*) Somebody did research on the remains of that bordello that was found. It was a Victorian house that was moved somewhere when they tore down Bunker Hill. The house had a garden and a wrap-around porch, so the men could wait pleasantly for their turn. All the girls' portraits hung in the hallway, painted in their Victorian gowns and curls. Mulholland used to go there, and all the silent movie stars. People might think it was a hard lifestyle for the girls. But maybe the men all treated them well and the girls were happy. Although. A young woman's skeleton was found, near the foundation remains. It looked as if she had been buried in the yard. I wonder what happened to her. (*Pause.*) Perhaps, after entertaining a group of men with her body, she wandered away. Nobody saw her go outside, and maybe it was unusually cold that night in

Los Angeles. And they found her frozen in the yard, the next day.

(*He turns and walks away, up the hill toward the observatory.*)

The End

Your Husband's Friend

by Sharon Yablon

Your Husband's Friend *was presented in front of a garage by Sharon's Farm, August 2012. It was directed by the playwright with the following cast:*

KEVIN   *Brad Culver*
MARLA   *Corryn Cummins*

Setting

Marla's backyard in the home she shared with her ex-husband in the San Fernando Valley; Saturday afternoon. The play takes place in front of Marla's open garage.

(MARLA *is barefoot in a house dress, near an open garage. Boxes of things are nearby. She stares off. KEVIN stands near the ivy, looking at her. He gets closer.*)

Kevin   You should install a gate. Anyone can walk back here. But I knew that before I tried it. (*He enters more, looks at her stuff. He picks something up.*) Is this one of those Easter Island heads?

Marla   It's a tumbler.

Kevin   But you didn't go there, did you? Armchair traveler? (*Pause.*) Hey, what was the deal there anyway? They ate themselves right off the island and they should have known better. (*He spies something.*) Your cat looks dead.

Marla   He's 18.

Kevin   It must cost a bundle to keep him alive.

Marla   I do what I have to do. Even though. He's not the same cat.

Kevin   What do you mean? Is he possessed? (*He laughs at his joke.*)

Marla   Our personalities get worse as we get older. We change.

Kevin   Change?

Marla   We become unrecognizable, horrible. Although the seeds were always there.

(*Pause.*)

Kevin   Have you gone through the death of a pet yet? One day you won't be able to find your cat, because he's bleeding out, under your bed.

Marla	That cat lived with me in San Francisco, all through my twenties. I was promiscuous then and he knew it was the wrong choice for me.
Kevin	That's cool. Well. I was just in the neighborhood.
Marla	Is that so?
Kevin	And thought I'd come by. How are you doing Marla?
Marla	Fine.
Kevin	(*Disbelieving.*) Oh really. (*Pause.*) Borders is having a going out of business sale! People are like vultures. I picked up a shitload of John Grisham, some Pat Conroy—
Marla	Pat Conroy?
Kevin	Yeah, you know "Beach Music," "The Prince of Tides." He's a Southern guy.
Marla	I know who he is, I thought mostly women read him.
Kevin	Have you read him?
Marla	No.
Kevin	Well, that's wrong then. I picked up "The Planet of the Apes" box set for $11.99! That's like six movies! You know it could happen, apes getting language. I bolted down my new entertainment center, I'm earthquake proof and ready to go! You'll have to come over and see my new Toshiba flat screen TV. It's a 55 inch Plasma display. The new compatible Bluetooth 3-D glasses aren't available yet, but I can TiVo whatever you want. What are your favorite shows?
Marla	I don't have any.
Kevin	Marla, what are you saying? (*Takes a step towards her.*) Do you need somebody to be on suicide watch for you? (*Pause.*) I went on Zoloft after my divorce. Are you on Facebook? I went on that after my divorce too.

Marla	No.
Kevin	You're kidding, right? It's so awesome! I can find people I've lost.
Marla	You mean people who didn't want to keep in touch with you?
Kevin	Anyway, I can see what everyone's up to.
Marla	What's everyone up to?

(*Pause.*)

Kevin	They're having a Mel Brooks festival on TCM starting tonight. I'll have to tape them all because I have plans. "Young Frankenstein" is tonight at 7:00, then "Silent Movie" tomorrow. They're showing "History of the World Part 1 and 2" back to back on Friday which is good because they really shouldn't be separated. When Madeline Kahn had those multiple orgasms, that's an urban legend, right?
Marla	I get them.
Kevin	No way! What are they like? Do you run out of breath or forget you're hungry?

(*Pause.*)

| Marla | I was lying. |

(*Pause.*)

Kevin	Why would you do that?
Marla	I don't know.

(He stares at her, it's hard to read his mood. He looks at records in a box.)

Kevin   Loggins and Messina, CSNY, yeah I had all these. Anything that would put a woman in the mood! Why did I give all my records away? Bread, wow! (*Sings.*) I found her diary underneath a tree, and started reading about me. (*Stops singing, keeps looking.*)

Who's Patti Smith?

(She stares at him.)

Kevin   (*Stumbling.*) Right, Patti Smith. (*Examines a nearby juicer, condescendingly.*) I have the Jack LaLanne Power Juicer. It's a sleek, compact design and has a non-drip spout. There's a surgical quality to its blades. Have you seen the infomercial? The actors are pretty good. Most people who decide to start juicing do so because they want to make a change—

Marla   I don't want to drink my food.

Kevin   Yeah, people who juice everything are weird! I have a Magic Bullet too. I wouldn't say I'm 100% satisfied. For instance, it doesn't froth milk for a cappuccino. (*Thinks.*) Wait a minute, this is all Dan's stuff.

Marla   I'm selling it.

Kevin   But I guess I can pretend I didn't see this. I wouldn't think Dan would settle for a mediocre juicer when he has embossed business cards... did he ever get that Frontgate umbrella that electronically moves with the sun?

Marla	He took it with him.
Kevin	Well, you've got more sunshine back here now! Get your Vitamin D! Have you been to his condo yet? It's the Los Feliz Towers? They're nice but half of the patios face their twin tower. You can call that a view, but I won't.
Marla	His doesn't.
Kevin	Oh. You've been there?
Marla	He had a housewarming party.
Kevin	(*Trying to disguise hurt that he wasn't invited.*)

I commend you for going but don't think you're fooling anyone. Parties. I mean, everyone has an agenda. You trying to prove something, Dan showing off, the women all hate each other, everyone wants to get laid. People have to drink because they don't know how to talk to each other. (*Pause.*) I owe him a phone call. Maybe he's annoyed? People in L.A. don't tell you when they're pissed, they just disappear from your life. I want to ask about that umbrella... you'll keep finding things of his, but don't think you can use them or get a decent price off eBay. Lori left a bum printer and some books, "The Joy Luck Club," yeah thanks, I'll *never* read that piece of shit! "The Artist's Way," what a colossal wank! I went right to the Iliad, you know that bookstore on Cahuenga? Traded in all her shit and got some of my own. (*Pause.*) So are you getting back to the old you? I sure had to change some habits when I got married.

I won't go into detail, but you can guess and you'd be right!

Marla	I came to hate Dan, but I do miss a body next to me. It can be an animal or even a woman, and the other night it was. I went to "She," a girl bar in Studio City.

Kevin	Tell me more!
Marla	It's in a building that sells carpets during the day.
Kevin	Wow!
Marla	That's like any club.
Kevin	Oh.
Marla	I didn't know much about the lesbian underworld.
Kevin	There are some real lesbian *dogs*! They're so ugly men won't touch them and they had to become gay.
Marla	People don't become gay. They're born gay.
Kevin	Yeah, I don't think so.
Marla	Sometimes a person has two sex organs, and the circus is their only home. Or they'll look at themselves in the mirror and see an incomplete person, so they need to cut off a limb. It's a very hard predicament for their partner to be in. Some people are attracted to stuffed animals, and some people want to be one.
Kevin	Yeah, let's just cut to the chase at the lesbo club.
Marla	I sat at the bar and it was a few minutes before anyone talked to me, but I didn't feel like shit like I do at straight bars.
Kevin	(*Disparaging.*) I bet the Indigo Girls or Joni Mitchell was playing.
Marla	A woman bought me a drink. She had breast cancer and wore a wig but I didn't find that out until later... a smooth, bald head running its tongue up and down my body, with the moonlight coming in through the window. We can't know what our future will be. (*Pause.*) The bald head could have belonged to Sean Connery or Bruce Willis.
Kevin	Or Sinead O'Connor, she was hot!

Marla	But it was Sherri's and she didn't care if I had a big bush because she values a woman's body.
Kevin	You're hairy?
Marla	I'm Russian.
Kevin	I didn't know that. Well, yeah it's nice to be valued but it'll come time to go *down* and pay the piper! I wouldn't mind seeing some girl-on-girl. It's on the bucket list—
Marla	What do you want, Kevin?
Kevin	Anything up for grabs here?

(*She gestures yes.*)

Kevin	I'll take the Bread record. (*Takes it.*) And I saw *The Power of Now,* I'll take that too.
Marla	The whole book is the title so you don't have to read it.
Kevin	Do you have any lemonade or anything?
Marla	No.
Kevin	Hey, have you caught that shit fetish video that's been going around e-mail? My dentist had it on his phone. (*Pause.*) Well I'm sure Dan will regret his decision.
Marla	People don't change their minds after they leave someone. That only happens in movies.
Kevin	So what have you been up to? (*Pause.*) How about that, swim class? (*Approaches her.*) I'll catch you. I'll catch up to you, if you lie.
Marla	I'm taking a swim class.
Kevin	Good. You know. The gravel on the driveway has seared the tips of my fingers. For I was crawling you see. A group of children followed me. I told them things I could never tell anybody. I spat at them. Spat words out at

	them. The words fell from my mouth in patterns. On the gravel driveway, that leads up to your house...
Marla	Lori and I are getting certified together.
Kevin	Jolly! What do you talk about? Her failed lymphatic massage business? Her repressed memories?
Marla	Don't make light of a painful situation; it makes you small.
Kevin	Whoa, that's deep! Like that *Twilight Zone* where all the evil people shrink at four o'clock! She's a sphincter! A parallel universe split off from the mother ship! She's an owl's raw rodent breath, a terrible temple of a fearful god, a demon's DNA. She's oily, garlicky, sunburst, snow-blind. She's foot cheese.
Marla	Kevin, your behavior has deteriorated and I'd like you to wait quietly in the yard.

(*He goes to the yard.*)

Marla	He did, at first. Minded me, at first. In the quiet world. Something is changing. There are cracks in the sky. Cuddle me. Massage me you dummy. I let his words soil me. My life fell away from me then. Should a person just stop eating and see what happens? I want to glide by the people I've hurt. Our marriage is in trouble. We'll travel, you said. In a boat somewhere. Ancient islands, thrust up. The sweat from your skin coats me and we fuck on the ruins. We never speak of it but we know it is the last time.
Kevin	I have sexual things I want to try with a wife. I'm frightened. Marla? (*Comes back.*) It's Saturday.

Marla	I know.
Kevin	How are you doing?
Marla	I'm fine.
Kevin	Good.
Marla	Are you okay, Kevin?
Kevin	There's a sale... I've been seeing Sasha! She's a Land's End model.
Marla	Does that make you feel good?
Kevin	It makes me feel bad. She has cocaine breath. She gets none of my jokes, and you know me.
Marla	Yes, you like to make people laugh. But you're not funny and you need to accept your limitations.
Kevin	I'm not funny? You never told me that before.
Marla	It's not easy to tell someone the truth about themselves. I'm telling you now.
Kevin	Marla?
Marla	Yes.
Kevin	What are you up to?
Marla	I'm getting rid of Dan's things.
Kevin	I still can't believe I'm divorced! I just got in the car and drove... what's with this swim class? You and my wife? Marla?
Marla	We're getting certified.
Kevin	Certified? That's looking at coral? What are you going to do with this house? Shouldn't you change it? Shouldn't we change things after they leave? (Pause) I remember us looking for houses together, me and my wife. She liked Spanish style and they all had this bougainvillea. You know that plant isn't even from here?!
Marla	A lot of people who live here aren't from here.

Kevin	The lack of seasons here keeps you fixed in time... it was my father's money that I was going to use to buy the house, but the realtors didn't know that. They treated me with respect...
Marla	It could have been your money. If you had discovered your potential.

(*He goes to her.*)

Kevin	Can people be replaced?
Marla	No.
Kevin	What is dating?
Marla	It's blotting the last person out with new people. Eventually the brain will try to conjure up a face, but it won't remember.
Kevin	Be careful, married people told me. Don't get too cushy. There are no guarantees. May I come closer? There are children in their beds, without mothers. The mothers have gone, left the families. Neighborhoods are changing. Draw the curtains... so Marla, did you like being married?
Marla	I did.
Kevin	What was a typical day like?
Marla	It's all blurred together now.
Kevin	Do you think I'll see my wife again? Ever again? How can that be?
Marla	If we had children, we could focus on them. Forget about ourselves, and focus on them...
Kevin	Our investments didn't pan out.
Marla	I don't think you have any.

Kevin	Dan hasn't returned my calls.
Marla	He's not going to.
Kevin	I don't like my life.
Marla	People can smell it. It brings them down.
Kevin	We went to the Bowl. The four of us. Restaurants. For years... were we all friends, or was it just convenient?

(*Pause, they stare at each other. She looks away.*)

Marla	Hatfields and the Water Grill. Jar and Cut. Tables around the pool, or with a view. Aged rib eyes and wild caught salmon. Things were going well. But then they weren't and nobody wants to hear about that. It makes the Caesar salad taste bad. My father had esophageal cancer and I kept it light at the restaurants. We talked about nothing and it was great! Lori left you, nobody wants to hear about that. You don't know what to do, nobody wants to hear about that. You don't have a life without her, didn't have a back up plan if she were to leave... my husband left me and I have friends because I don't talk about it. And we go to movies and art openings. Clubs and dinner parties. I'm rarely alone. My father died and nobody knew. Especially my friends.
Kevin	I'm sorry about your father. (*He goes to hug her.*) Want to fuck? I didn't mean. I'm sorry. (*He breaks away from her.*)
Marla	What? I'm nice, I'm not fat. What's wrong with me?!
Kevin	(*Softly.*) Nothing.

(*Pause.*)

Marla	I would lie there naked next to him. And he didn't do a thing. He stopped touching me. A long time ago.
Kevin	I'm sorry. (*Pause.*) Having all this time now, to do what I want. Is strange.
Marla	You're single! (*Said with false enthusiasm.*)
Kevin	But I have sexual things I want to try with my wife. Look what I've done to my hands...

(*She takes his hands and looks down at them. His eyes follow and they stay like this for the rest of the play.*)

Marla	They're beautiful.
Kevin	Marla. Are you saying that we'll recover from people? From losing them?
Marla	I don't think we can.
Kevin	What's dating?
Marla	Blotting the person you love out.
Kevin	There's a sale. I have to go to Radio Shack. And then I don't know what else I'll do. Why don't you have favorite shows?
Marla	I don't know.
Kevin	I'll call Dan.
Marla	Don't. He was never really your friend. We all just did stuff together.
Kevin	I'll call my wife.
Marla	She's gone.
Kevin	*Young Frankenstein* is on tonight. It's Saturday in Los Angeles! I have my health. I can see the giant boulder at LACMA. I can blade at the beach. It's beautiful outside! Boy, Culver City has really started to boom! The Valley

is huge! Is it okay to park overnight here, or do I need a permit? How are you doing anyway, Marla? How are you *really* doing? Did you get all the things you ever wanted?

(*Their eyes meet one another's.*)

Kevin   Tell me. I am your husband's friend... (*He sort of crumbles in her arms, she consoles him.*)

The End

Plan B

by Gray Palmer

Plan B *was produced by Padua Playwrights as part of* The Hive Project *at the University of Notre Dame, October 2013. It featured music by Gray Palmer, which he performed on guitar with April Guthrie on cello. The play was directed by the playwright with the following cast:*

JACK   *Max Faugno*
EDITH   *Alana Dietze*

Characters

JACK, *a depressed labor organizer.*
EDITH, *a virgin queen bee who has assumed human form.*

Setting

They are performing onstage for the audience.

(*An empty space. Musicians sit at the side of the stage, visible to the audience. The actors may place two chairs onstage mid-way through the performance. The performance should begin with music to accompany the entrance of* JACK *and* EDITH.)

Jack I don't want to be human any more. Knowing what I know. When I expressed this wish, someone heard it. *Zukunftspoesie*! This is the first page of the prophetic book. I don't look different, do I? I still have two legs. My rods and cones remain on the inside of my eyeballs, and so on. Yes. But. I'm a new form. In relation and action. A mutation like this—I don't want an argument; it's not a *conversion*, it's horizontal mutation. A mutation in the head takes time to become visible. In relation and action. As to distribution through the population? That's why we're here. This is my understanding as a forerunner. We're a group of people at an infectious "performance." Yes. But what is that? It's a process of chemosensory interaction. Future people may watch this on a device of archive retrieval. And I greet them. Future people, I greet you! They may be moved. But can they smell us? No. We, however, we are changed. This is a performance of the prophetic book. This is the first page.

None of this is my idea. Look, my friend wants to make a brood comb out of you. And plant a series of eggs. We can say that. Yes. She says, Man is malleable.

Edith Man is malleable.

Jack	She says, Man has been made and re-made many times without knowing how or why.
Edith	How? Why?
Jack	I do ask, Why me as index case? Why me as progenitor of a future hybrid? I have asked that. There appear to be reasons. Rarity of occurrence, unusual pre-adaptation, and so on. I don't know; I leave it to the scholars.
Edith	Three nipples is a sign of virility, according to Ian Fleming.
Jack	What?
Edith	I fondly examine his teenage reading.
Jack	I'm not going to take off my shirt.
Edith	I saw him hiding in his basement.
Jack	She looks human, doesn't she? And why is she so interested in politics? We'll get to that.
	Since I discovered enhanced chemosensory communication, how can I put this...? Going back and forth across the inter-species border, aside from moments of nausea, on either side of the fold, there's a transitional view... I could compare it to airplane travel... I see a landscape below, from my little window, but the landscape is an incarnation... the different bodies I inhabit with different durations... Is affect itself the mode of travel...? Is it too much to say that? Affect, and by that I mean desire, is the same on both sides of the species fold... Desire. The transnational regulatory force! Desire and the drama of desire.
Edith	I told him to leave a jar outside.

Jack	I was afraid to go outside. I preferred to stay in the basement. After the political disaster. Thank god for Pink Dot.
Edith	Go ahead and explain what you know.
Jack	There's a bee in my basement. A virgin queen. A virgin queen who escaped the drone congregation area intact. She wants me to fill her spermatheca. So that she can create a new swarm. So that, in the future, a line of bees can fly through a curtain of fire.
Edith	A curtain of fire.
Jack	I don't have the proper intromittent organ. To say nothing about the problem of scale. But she's a scale-jumper.

How did I get here? That's a story. I was a taxi driver. Then I joined the steering committee of the workers alliance. The first meeting took place at a Denny's near the airport. I said, "Gen-zib kah-leh—bess-a mai ming-ged a-leh!" In Amharic that means, "Where there is money, there is a way in the sky." My pronunciation was bad. Also the leader of the alliance didn't expect to hear his language come from a face like mine. Right? So I had to repeat it. "Gen-zib kah-leh—bess-a mai ming-ged a-leh!" Then I passed a copy of Kapuscinski's book across the table. He looked at the first paragraph and said, "I know this dog. I've seen this dog." Lulu. The Emperor's dog. Within two months I was a member of the Board of Directors.

The first time I spoke on TV was at an Airport Commissioner's Meeting. *The Times* didn't quote me. They quoted Noah's inflammatory statement about bathrooms in the Holding Lot. But what I said was good for the men. And good for my safety. I said, "The fear of retaliation is real." And the men applauded. The next time I was at my company—the Russian company, the worst—the president asked me to shut the door. He said, "There will be no retaliation." Because I said it on TV. I thought they wouldn't discuss the lease-cap because they didn't understand it. The cap has to be attached to a fare increase. So if that moment passes, you're going to wait years for the next opportunity. It didn't matter if we couldn't win the proposal. We needed to make a public fight for it. That's how you organize the bottom. I argued this point right to the moment we typed the flyer with our policy statement.

Once I understood their position, I worried about what might happen "around the table" with a so-called worker representative and the Commissioners and owners. Yeah. I worried about that. What? Did I think I was Gramsci? Worker-councils were going to be set up at City Hall in Los Angeles? Public Utilities would be declared autonomous zones of the commonwealth? Enclosures off limits to commodification? And we would become a proto-labor party, federating with other municipal workers? Yes. Yes. I did imagine something like that. My political naïveté was appalling.

They ice-picked the tires of my taxi when I was paying the lease at the company. I had two flats on the 405 with a car full of passengers. Had to call a flatbed tow. One Russian at the airport would greet me as "Chapaev." A schoolbook hero of the Red Army. Or sometimes they would say to me, "Viva Cuba!" To these Russians, "union" equals the soviet. I studied their poets, too. "It is better to agonize than to organize," Brodsky.

Edith	I remember it better than you. Your efforts at socialist education.
Jack	Do you? Remind me.
Edith	You showed an obituary to the Eritrean driver, Paolos. And you explained about the bombing in Birmingham.
Jack	Oh, yeah.
Edith	What did he say?
Jack	Remind me.
Edith	He said, White people? They bombed the church? Eh? Were they Christians? Were the bombers Christians? But I thought they were supposed to hate Black people not Christians. So they would only bomb them if they were outside. This means they bombed them in front of Jesus Christ. No, that's bad. Right? That means they will be punished before God. Oh! Oh, this was a time when you had to get paper from owner before you could go out. He had to sign paper. Slavery. 1963. Logical.
Jack	That's exactly what he said. Isn't she amazing?
Edith	I quote from your palace of memory.
Jack	Political education takes time. Paolos was thinking of the French and the pass-laws in Djibouti. That's what he knew. He was trying to understand an atrocity. He has a *son* who loves to read.
Edith	Education takes time.
Jack	Show them one of your teaching songs.
Edith	The funny one?

Jack	Yeah.
Edith	Next I will teach you a song.
Jack	Oh, good.
Edith	Here are the lyrics. Repeat after me.
	You drive in a circle.
Jack	You drive in a circle.
Edith	Around a hole in your shadow.
Jack	Around a hole in your shadow.
Edith	With clotted hands.
Jack	With clotted hands.
Edith	You cannot lift a cup.
Jack	You cannot lift a cup.
Edith	Your stamping hoof is made of dung.
Jack	Say again?
Edith	Your stamping hoof is made of dung.
Jack	This is inspiring.
Edith	Yes, and it gets worse. In the next verse the world catches on fire. So tell us about your Lawrence of Arabia moment.
Jack	I put a necklace of taxis around City Hall and tightened it.
Edith	You were in the first car.
Jack	By default. I knew the route and the agreed-upon pace. I was at the clasp of the necklace. The president of the alliance had his permit revoked; otherwise it would have been him. There was a Chinese TV crew in my car. The reporter kept asking, "Are you disappointed?" No, because I didn't expect the city to act differently. I expected worse.

The Disaster! The men won't discuss a meter split. They refused to organize the workers who didn't own cars. Petty bourgeois car owners had captured the organization. I'm going to explain this one last time. Lease drivers rent their work. The car owners and taxi companies receive a fixed income, usually paid weekly, from driver gross earnings. The driver's income will be the difference after he makes this payment and subtracts fuel cost. The amount of the lease—and they are set high—is not regulated by the city of Los Angeles, though the city has the authority to do so. Typically, it can take 35 to 50 hours of driving to pay off a "full-time" lease. After that point, the driver begins to earn money. If a full-time lease-driver worked a mere forty-hour week, that driver would probably show a negative income. This employment structure explains why Los Angeles taxi drivers worked a median 72 hours a week in 2006. These conditions would be illegal to impose on employees, of course. But remember the sorcerer's pitch. Cab drivers are co-capitalists.

The lease system protects investor-owners from direct exposure to fluctuations of the business cycle and fuel cost, by pushing these elements of cost and risk onto the worker. What's it like to work under this arrangement?

You're the Boss of sleep deprivation. And here was the situation: the organization of drivers had been captured by owners. Landlordism. The principal means by which the urban poor monetize their equity is landlordism, often at the expense of even poorer people. The place and the formula were wrong. That's when I retired to the basement, drinking.

Edith	I came to your basement.
Jack	I could feel someone in the basement.
Edith	I said, How beautiful.
Jack	Something crackled on the shelf. I knew it was a message.
Edith	And then I crossed.
Jack	There was a beautiful, naked young woman in my basement. I put my shirt on her... My shirt on Edith became a robe—
Edith	Whose redness was more blazing than fire!
Jack	Along her sleeves were animated groves—
Edith	Of lupine, rosemary, and red currant.
Jack	A trim appeared—
Edith	Of huckleberry and the scorpion weed.
Jack	Collected grains dyed the cloth—
Edith	Of sage and Oregon grape. From desert colonies spread rings of creosote with local elderberry, rhododendron, and snowberry. And as the sun-compass of my people is most upright—purple coneflower, black-eyed susan, penstemon, and climax goldenrod. Light then declines to joe-pye weed and rabbitbrush, till in the lesser light the sisters feed on sleepy aster.
Jack	Five times across her robe—
Edith	A redness more blazing than fire!
Jack	Five times—
Edith	As my name is Edith. But language confused me.

Jack	When she tried to speak, there was a cloud of hexagons in the music.
Edith	Ooooo, aaaaaaaahhh, Ooooo, aaaaaaaahhh.
	We couldn't stay together long.
Jack	Why not?
Edith	But I could repeat my visit.
Jack	Something crackled on the shelf. And there was a tap at the window.
Edith	I could go back and I did. He was waiting.
Jack	How did she get upstairs?
Edith	I fly through a hole. I go through cracks in the masonry. Then I'm in the attic. And I come downstairs.
Jack	She was walking downstairs. Geometry was different around her.
Edith	I hadn't acquired speech yet. But I could dance.
Jack	Is it charades?
Edith	If I had been able to speak, these would have been the lyrics:
	You've got skin
	And your skin is smooth
	And a left side tan
	Your taxi tan
	When I was a girl
	I didn't know skin was smooth
	And I had no hand
Jack	If I'm going mad, it's not unpleasant.
Edith	Then—something of vital importance.
Jack	It's charades.
Edith	*Leave a jar on the windowsill.*
Jack	I understood that.

Edith	Then I vanished.
Jack	Part Two. The Translation.
Edith	When a bee becomes human, an archive is created.
Jack	When a man becomes bee, a stooge is illuminated.
Edith	He thought he was alone.
Jack	I was alone in my basement.
Edith	He doubted the status of my early visits.
Jack	I did.
Edith	That hurt.
Jack	I reviewed the political disaster. I tried to write an article for *Labor Notes*. It didn't go well. One day when I was reading—Hobsbawm, *The Social Bandit*—at about noon, the light in my room became strange. The basement window was covered with bees. Bees filled the window outside. They moved in waves and made ripples of light so that the basement looked like an aquarium.
Edith	He took naps. He usually slept on his left side. I was very quiet. I pulled apart the seams of his skull so that I could taste his higher language functions with my proboscis. And then at night, all night, the sisters rearranged his liquid in the combs. There's a lot of touching in the dark and each collision of the sisters was a logical operation. That is how I learned to speak so well.
Jack	I did have headaches.
Edith	We had our first conversation.
Jack	I didn't say anything.
Edith	I was over stimulated. I said, I adore reinforced concrete... Show me your tongue so that I can see red. Thank you. I have seen red... Jack, Jack, Jack-of-the-North, do you

	like my hair? But what if I were covered with bristles?
	What if I had hooks instead of hands...? My cousin can
	wrap *her* tongue around the top of her head like a turban.
	Can you bend your knees backward?
Jack	No.
Edith	That's OK... Does the hand/tool relation of human
	technology fascinate you? Do you have a knife? May
	I hold a knife?
Jack	Sure.
Edith	I'm a Robber Girl. I'm a queen on vacation pretending to
	be a Robber Girl. Show me your intromittent organ.
	Heigh-ho. Is it variable in size?
Jack	Usually.
Edith	For this misalliance to work, we need to avoid death by
	consummation. I'm checking for barbs. Smooth.
Jack	And then what happened did happen.
Edith	As we lay around like sacks of dirty water, I made my
	promise to Jack: if you fill my spermatheca on the other
	side—and you survive—I will share my secrets of social
	engineering. For the emancipation of both our species,
	I will do it in front of an audience.
Jack	She explained that we had to fashion an insect body for
	me. That was the purpose of the jar on the windowsill.
Edith	Have some jelly.
Jack	Feed me goo
	Oo oo oo
Edith	I have spoons on either side of my mouth
Jack	I like your goo
Edith	You love my Royal Jelly...
	Differential feeding triggers phenotypic expression.

Jack	Of jelly.
	Pack that goo
	Oo oo oo
	With the spoons on either side of your mouth
	I like your goo
Edith	You love my Royal Jelly.
	You may call me Edith, but this is my name.
	(*She spritzes him and he says the next two lines as though sneezing.*)
Jack	Witkiewicz!
Edith	Bless you.
Jack	Witkiewicz!
Edith	Bless you.
Jack	A vacancy was appearing in my mind. Discrete concepts were vanishing. Just before they became non-concepts, I wondered at their transparency. Money? What is money?
Edith	The commodity that expresses the universal equivalent value of all other commodities, poor thing.
Jack	My nostrils are closing up. I'm forgetting commodities. My nostrils are closing up and I'm forgetting the fictitious commodities!
Edith	It's working. Listen to the inner wind rushing across the fibrous membrane in my neck.
Jack	If we put this in the municipal water supply, will it abolish rent? Excuse me, my nostrils are closing up!
Edith	Listen to my voice. You are developing spiracles for respiration.
Jack	And I'm hot.
Edith	Bees don't sweat. Let me fan you during the transition. Jack, for the first fifteen minutes, you should avoid mirrors.

Jack	I'm trying to remember what are minutes.
Edith	Look at me. This long.
Jack	She's the intelligence of the organization.
Edith	You're traveling. We booked a room with a skylight for you. Don't leave the hotel. There are spider threads everywhere at night.
Jack	I waved to her through the fog. And I thought, The next time she stays over, I'm taking her to motocross. I love motocross. There suck I, there suck I, there suck I!
Edith	That is a fair account of Jack's departure for his first flight.
Jack	A drone is like riding a bucking mini-mecha.
Edith	You didn't stay in the hotel.
Jack	I went to the Speedway in the Forest.
Edith	We discovered that his endophallus is smooth on the other side. And he has turquoise armor.
Jack	That story is for another time. You may hear me tell it, if I survive. Now Edith is going to keep her promise.
Edith	Jack, Jack, Jack-of-the-North. I saw his face in a bag when he lifted the lid of the hive. He was helping the Keeper treat us for a mite infestation—the varroa destructor that brings white sickness. I thought, This is a god with his head in a bag. He can save us from the curtain of fire. My scouts found him. Jack. There will be a curtain of fire.
Jack	There will be a curtain of fire.
Edith	Now, Humans, I pull out the golden nail in your head. Now, Humans, of lumpen-liberal variety, I dissolve your clot.

	The surplus is available to all.
Jack	The surplus is available to all.
Edith	My prophecy is simple.
	There will be a curtain of fire.
	Divide the hive and go to a new home.
	The location is determined by swarm.
	It will be in a luminous vacancy!
	I have two specific recommendations.
	Replace the Joint Chiefs of Staff with women.
Jack	That's obvious.
Edith	Seize Lockheed Martin and reconfigure it with projects to halt the damage of the Anthropocene.
Jack	Put up your dukes!
Edith	The Wheel of Labor is radiant and varied, but I favor public transportation and urban agriculture. Fight for the New Hybrid!
Jack	Fight for the New Hybrid!
Edith	Prepare the federation of resistance!
Jack	Prepare the federation of resistance!

The End

Amber

by Rachel Jendrzejewski

Amber *was produced by Padua Playwrights as part of* The Hive Project *at the University of Notre Dame, October 2013. It featured music by Theo Goodell and Sarah Holtschlag. The play was directed by Laurie Woolery with the following cast:*

FIGURE 1   *Corryn Cummins*
FIGURE 2   *Alana Dietze*

Characters

FIGURE 1
FIGURE 2

> *Both are female and sing*
> *with and without words.*

Setting

Everything takes place outside of time.

Music

The songs and movement don't rush,
but they're very present, electric, magnetic.

(Sound of a musical saw
Two female figures in separate spaces
Their movement is a hexagonal chess game)

Fig. 1 & 2 (*singing*)

Amber won't dance for us anymore

Amber won't dance for us anymore

Amber won't dance for us anymore

Amber won't dance for us anymore

Fig. 1 I don't know where I am when I wake up

Dull ache, upper right

Pressure

I pull myself out and make

geometries

with my hands

all morning long

that's work, you know

In the afternoons

I become a network of roots

and find myself thinking about

honey

Not anxiously

it's just a persistent

drip

By dusk

I look over at Amber

lying stretched

across a plane

unmoving

Oh Amber

We influence each other
She has a heart-shaped head
In the late evening
I untangle myself and make tea
hot and black, no honey
We make our way through silent speeches
and think about the world
all the big things going on in the world
Oh world
Oh Amber
We situate ourselves
near each other
I ask her all the most pressing questions
She answers by way of scent
Wise Amber, or cowardly
sometimes it's difficult to know which
but she gets away with it
And this is how we go about
the act of
disappearing

(*FIG. 2 sings a song without words*
She sounds like the saw)

Fig. 1   They look at us like we're divine
Fig. 2   If only they knew
         We talk to each other
Fig. 1   In our own way
Fig. 2   Amber used to fly over me at night

It was all I could do to keep both feet on the ground

Fig. 1 We're taking all of mathematics with us
You wasteful—

Fig. 2 Honey
Unadulterated
No bits of lead, metal
chloramphenicol
disclosure
Amber knows the ideal most efficient way
to partition a plane into equal areas
Elaborate wallpaper patterns, she laughs
We have no place in time

Fig. 1 Time's got nothing to offer us
Just wait until they find out, squinting
words don't mean anything at all
Not really

Fig. 2 We keep our eyes on the work
Fig. 1 Timely labor
Fig. 2 Amber likes fresh air and current events
things agreed to be relevant
important and happening now,
exciting and horrible

Fig. 1 Passing is always soon
We're not sleeping these days
which is the root of most problems

Fig. 2	Which in fact means we're sleeping all the time
	You see how that works
	Artificial light threw everyone for a loop
	and now we have this traveling salesman problem
	It's embarrassing
	Pure mechanism
	I have a vision of the whole that can't be shared

Fig. 1   Humiliation
Amber won't dance for us anymore
Her brain is the size of a seed of grass
Birds navigate the sky by memorizing star patterns
but she—
but we—

Fig. 2   We are taking all of mathematics with us
Starting with
Honey

(*She draws on the floor with chalk*)

$$A = \frac{3\sqrt{3}}{2}\,t^2 \approx 2.598076211t^2$$

Fig. 1   I'm not an expert
but I do find myself a little breathless over that one

Fig. 2   You don't know
Fig. 1   We don't know

It's a certain condition which knows

Fig. 2   You're out of book

Fig. 1   Honey
They will no doubt ask
what constitutes a problem

Fig. 2   A king and a rook can checkmate a lone king
A king and two bishops can checkmate a lone king
A king and two knights can checkmate a lone king
A king and a bishop and a knight can checkmate a lone king

Fig. 1   But where has the queen gone?

Fig. 2   We take her for granted

Fig. 1   Amber always misunderstood thinking
She would say it's unproblematic business
But truth changes what we think
And our thoughts change truth
It's very problematic
It has incredible ramifications

Fig. 2   We used to live there together, Amber and I
Together we lived and worked
In a live-work space
Convenient and full of amenities
Raw in appearance, but not raw really

Fig. 1   We make sure nothing's too raw

Fig. 2	Quiet positions
Fig. 1	Wild tactics
Fig. 2	We're melting cities slowly, you see
	We'll be gone before anyone notices
Fig. 1 & 2	(*Singing*)
	Amber won't dance for us anymore
	Amber won't dance for us anymore
	Amber won't dance for us anymore
	Amber won't dance for us anymore
Fig. 1	Identities don't come before difference
	Being is difference
	Isn't that what they say?
	Reality is a body without organs
	Reality is a body without skin
	Reality is pure honey
Fig. 2	Oh world
	Oh Amber
	We've been fooling ourselves this whole time
Fig. 1	Reason is always a region
Fig. 2	Geographic
Fig. 1	No
Fig. 2	Reality is always a rhizome
Fig. 1	Holographic
Fig. 2	No
Fig. 1	Underneath it all lies delirium and drift
Fig. 2	Yes

Fig. 1	Honey is creation
Fig. 2	Honey is creation
	Bodies are simply
	different ways to organize the flux,
	let's say
Fig. 1	Herein lies the secret:
	to bring into existence and not judge
Fig. 2	But we know something more than Amber
Fig. 1	We're an effect, not a cause
Fig. 1 & 2	(*Singing*)
	Amber won't dance for us anymore
Fig. 1	We know that speaking is a way of doing
Fig. 2	We know that speaking is a way of performing actions
Fig. 1	But we speak through scent
Fig. 2	We don't really speak at all, per say
Fig. 1	We speak through scent
Fig. 2	We don't really speak at all
Fig. 1 & 2	(*Singing*)
	Amber won't dance for us anymore
Fig. 2	We know that performance doesn't mean what she thinks
Fig. 1	This is serious business
Fig. 2	This is life or death
Fig. 1	Becoming produces nothing other than itself
Fig. 1 & 2	(*Singing*)
	Amber won't dance for us anymore

Fig. 2

I don't know where I am when I wake up

Dull ache, upper right

Pressure, buzzing

I hold my face

I like to think of it as a complete body

My face, a complete body

All night long

that's work, you know

In the cracks of days

I close my eyes and become honey

find myself thinking about

our home

our small spaces of sleep

home is sleep, is it not

We sleep all the time

That's the problem

We're home more than we think

We make ourselves busy inside

Periodically

I look over at Amber

lying stretched

across a plane

unmoving

Oh Amber and that heart-shaped head

We hate each other, really

I make hot black tea, no honey,

pour it through her legs

Her inactive bent legs

We make our way through silent speeches

and of course we're both thinking about the world

all the big things going on in the world

the wars, the health problems, the chemicals

Oh world

Oh Amber

You know it's not our fault

But it is

But it's not

But it is

But it's not

We go back and forth

I situate myself near her

She doesn't move

I ask her all the most pressing questions:

Dear Amber, what do you make of it?

Dear Amber, what are we to do with ourselves?

Dear Amber, why the long face?

Why didn't you say anything before, Amber?

Why won't you say anything now?

She answers by way of scent

I can't stand her in these moments

She never gives a straight answer

But it doesn't matter anyway

We're melting cities slowly, you see

We'll be gone before anyone notices

(*She draws on the walls, the floor, every available space with chalk*)

$$A = \frac{3\sqrt{3}}{2} t^2 \approx 2.598076211 t^2$$

(*FIG. 1 sings a song without words*
She sounds like the saw)

Fig. 1   Before the regime of signs
           After the regime of signs
           Whole bodies of people
           falling onto the ground
           into the sea
           disappearing
           fingers snapping

Fig. 2   I'm slow
           I'm sorry
           The world is fixed timber
           Falling

Fig. 1   Amber might say
           depersonalize through love, not subjection

Fig. 2   Amber might say
           we're blocks of becoming

Fig. 1   What's anyone to do with that?
Fig. 2   What "anyone"?
           Who's anyone?

Fig. 1   These are everyday concerns
Fig. 2   Ideas are always reusable
           New contexts

Fig. 1	To some extent
Fig. 2	The math is very simple
	Nobody needs to study beyond geometry
	if that

Fig. 1	I'm not content to proceed by resemblance
	I'm not a series
	You're not a series

Fig. 2	We are not progressing or regressing along a series
Fig. 1 & 2	(*Singing with the saw*)

Amber won't dance for us anymore
Amber won't dance for us anymore
Amber won't dance for us anymore
Amber won't dance for us anymore
Amber won't dance for us anymore
Amber won't dance for us anymore
Amber won't dance for us anymore
Amber won't dance for us anymore
Amber won't dance for us anymore
Amber won't dance for us anymore
Amber won't dance for us anymore
Amber won't dance for us anymore
Amber won't dance for us anymore
Amber won't dance for us anymore
Amber won't dance for us anymore
Amber won't dance for us anymore
Amber won't dance for us anymore
Amber won't dance for us anymore

Amber won't dance for us anymore
Amber won't dance for us anymore
Amber won't dance for us anymore
Amber won't dance for us anymore
Amber won't dance for us anymore
Amber won't dance for us anymore

(*As they sing, their words dissolve into sound without
words*
They become bees, circling, then disappearing
We hear only their voices
then the saw
then silence)

The End

Hello, Say

by Guy Zimmerman

An earlier version of Hello, Say *was produced by Padua Playwrights as part of* The Hive Project, *at the Society of Literature, Science and the Arts conference at Notre Dame, October 2013. The play featured original music composed and performed by cellist by April Guthrie. It was directed by the playwright, with the following cast:*

JOHN   *Gray Palmer*
CLARA   *Corryn Cummins*

Characters

JOHN	*Fifties, a wealthy American engineer and businessman.*
BERNARDO	*Forties, a psychologist and assassin.*
CANDY	*Thirties, a former customer service employee for an airline.*
CLARA	*A former lover of JOHN, to be played by the same actor as CANDY.*

Setting

A domestic interior in a suburb of L.A., late at night. This is the living room of Candy's house. The room can be evoked with an armchair and a side table only, and with an implied entrance to an adjacent kitchen nearby.

(LIGHTS *up on* JOHN, *seated in the armchair , a* MAN'S
CAP *on the side table nearby.* BERNARDO *is beside the
chair.* CANDY *stands facing them, a short distance
away.* JOHN *wears jean shorts with long pant legs
and a windbreaker. His shins are bruised.* BERNARDO
is in a guayabera. CANDY *wears a dressing gown. Both
men are dirty and disheveled. The* SOUND *of many
clocks.*)

John	(*To* CANDY) That perfume you're wearing, I bet it has some fucked up name. And I bet you love it. Saying it. That name. To a friend, say. You're out with a group of yas, out for lunch. You do that, right? Lunch? Sure, you do. It's like your major occupation. Lunch, perfume, shops where they sell clothes. Nice things. You love nice things. And talking about nice things. And I love you for it. To me it's full of mystery. And sickness. That's what you are to me. Mystery and sickness. Done up with a bow.
Bernardo	Do you live here alone?
Candy	Alone, yeah. 'Cept for—
John	So it's private here? We have privacy?
Bernardo	You got a lot of clocks, lady.
Candy	You noticed that.
Bernardo	Almost like a collection.
John	I had a girlfriend had a lot of clocks. Well, she wasn't *my* girlfriend exactly, if you know what I mean. But I find it surprising. In the sense that talking to you by phone I pictured an office somewhere not this house with clocks.

How about you, Bernie? What did you imagine when I told you about Candy?

Bernardo   An office.

John   With cubicles, right?

Bernardo   And tables.

John   Instead it's like this *house*. (*Pause. Clock ticking.*) Are you scared, Candy? Afraid?

Candy   A little.

John   I can see why you might be. Two men arriving like we did, unannounced and with big grins. Out of the weather. (*Long pause. Clocks tick.*) Don't worry, though. I can be gentle. You can talk to my girlfriend who liked clocks. I had interviews. In the business monthlies. The Genius of the Year they called me. With my anti-virus software—I was ahead of the curve. That was 1995, '96, somewhere in there. You can read my interviews and behold a gentle spirit. But then I—

(*Pause.*)

Candy   What?

John   Excuse me?

Candy   What happened to you then?

John   (*Pause.*) I have these moments where I... What happened to me? What it was... I fell. I fell all the way. That became my life. One long fall. One long tumble. It was the very best I could do, see. The very best. You.

Candy   What about me?

John	I was looking for you.

(*Pause.*)

Candy	There are caves I could take you to. You might learn something. I can tell you're thinking about me. Both of you. My eyes. My neck. I have a long neck, I know. Like a tall bird. These caves, they're full up with garbage. People put all kinda trash up there. Mattresses, chandeliers, whole cars. Fancy cars like Mercedes and big old V-8s—Mustangs, Chevelles. I don't care about cars. (*To JOHN*) Shiiiit. How come you got them bruises? I bet it's *medical* problems. We could go at night up there. I'll show you the paths back to the old caves. Back up in there to where the bees used to be.
John	(*Pointing*) Who's the cap belong to, Candy?

(*Pause.*)

Candy	Bud. That's Bud's cap.
Bernardo	Where's Bud now?
Candy	Off somewhere. Can I offer you some food? (*Indicating kitchen door.*) You can help yourself to whatever.
John	Bernie, go help yourself to some food.
Bernardo	Down in the jungle Mr. John gave me a job to build him a wall against the sea. A sea wall. He pay up front for half, but then the soldiers came.
John	He's Guatemalan, Bernie.

Bernardo	Soldiers say "Your Mr. John, he shoot a man. Please come with us."
John	Bernie's not his real name: Bernardo.
Bernardo	Mr. John say, "here, soldiers, have some pepper spray for your eyes," and into the jungle we go.
John	He's a paid assassin. Also a psychologist.
Bernardo	We catch a bus. We steal a nice truck.
John	Bernardo helps me make sense of my issues in life.
Bernardo	We stop in this crazy bar—all of a sudden here we are with you and all your many clocks.
John	This doesn't have to end badly, Candy. Nothing does.
Bernardo	I don't know if I'm dressed all right or not.
John	Nothing needs to end badly. We can have dignity, can't we? We can even be a light for each other, why not.
Candy	(*To* BERNARDO.) It's okay for in here, how you're dressed.
Bernardo	I could use a fresh t-shirt maybe. Unisex.
John	Bernie told you about the sea wall—what he didn't tell you is he got paid good money to kill me. Right, Bernie?
Bernardo	Right, Chief.
John	Six guys over the last couple years have been paid good money to kill me—I hired them all away. Thugs, killers and whores make the best company. But we're not here to talk about me. We are here to talk about you. And your work with the airlines. A customer service position—which means you are supposed to serve the needs of the consumer, Candy.

(BERNARDO *exits toward the kitchen. Silence.*)

Candy	You think I don't know who you are? You think I don't remember? The flight you missed and the connection out of Chicago that—
John	Do not.
Candy	(*Pause.*) It was my first week on the job that time you called. With your flight cancellation problems.
John	All the lives you could have lived.
Candy	For five hours you kept me on the line.
John	But now it's only this one life.
Candy	And still you were not satisfied.
John	And all of it comes down to this.
Candy	"That sick fucker will come into your life" said Bud when I told him about it.
John	I've always frightened people and I've never known why.
Candy	"With his tangled-up heart."
John	But I knew it could make me lots of money.
Candy	When you're on the phone for five hours I guess you get entangled with each other.
John	You called me a psychopath. On the phone that time when we met.
Candy	I remember that, sure.

(BERNARDO *re-enters, eating a juicy peach.* JOHN *stands. Steps toward* CANDY. *Stops.*)

John	You said I had at least five of the six defining characteristics. Of a psychopath. You said you could tell just from my voice. Is that fair?
Bernardo	(*Chewing.*) A hand grenade with the pin pulled out—would you call it an opportunity? (*Taking a*

	bite of peach.) That's the first question I ask all my patients.
John	(*To Candy.*) You said there was no point being polite to a psychopath like me because psychopaths don't care one way or another. That was smart. That was a smart thing to say. And I decided to come introduce myself.
Candy	All the way from Honduras.
John	Belize.
Candy	You said you lived in Honduras.
John	I was lying.
Candy	Why would you lie to me about something like that?
John	I forgot why. Do you always have that effect on people?
Candy	No but Bud does. That's his cap. He has terrible scars. Facial scars. You'd think maybe it was from acne but no. It's plague. Black plague. Bubonic plague. He caught it working on the reservations. The prairie dogs are vectors for plague. Bud almost died but then he didn't. You could wear his cap. No? That's okay. Tell me something—when we first spoke on the phone… was it my voice you fell in love with?
John	I told you everything at that time.
Candy	Tell me again.
John	"Someone will have to die because of this," is what I told you.
Candy	You're here because you want revenge, yes.
John	I was flying en route to a funeral and I missed it because of you and your idiot airline.
Candy	But now you also *want* me.
John	Funeral of an old friend. My old friend Joe.

Candy	I bet you want a kiss on the lips—well forget it.
John	There was someone I wanted to see at the funeral. She never forgave me for missing it. Clara. It was my one chance to get back with her. Back with Clara.
Candy	Okay, then I'm sorry I hung up on you.
John	Do you know what it's like to be haunted by a woman, Candy? Of course not.
Candy	And I'm sorry I routed you through Phoenix out of spite.
John	Bernie knows. Don't you, Bernie?
Candy	It's becoming for me hard to talk right, I need to warn you.
John	It's me.
Candy	Like I have a wire twisted my in brain. What's you?
John	That you can't talk right. It's something I thought up and now it's happening for real. I have these special powers, I think.
Candy	Too I have them.
John	(*To* CANDY.) Excuse me. (*Then, to* BERNARDO.) Bernie... Bernie.... I'm a little dizzy now... is there room by that TV...? Help me over to the chair, Bernie... Help...

(BERNARDO *helps* JOHN *to the chair.* CANDY *laughs. A* CELLO *sounds. Brief tableaux.*)

Bernardo	He has these spells. He's not that healthy.

(JOHN *leans back, passing out. A pause.* CANDY *crosses to a window. Looks out.*)

What is it?

Candy	A memory. Random. A day. The light. On the street and traffic. A big city. I think I'm becoming somebody different. Someone from out of John's past, a person he truly loved. As we go to the caves.
Bernardo	What happens when we die?
Candy	A world comes to an end.
Bernardo	A world...
Candy	Does that surprise you? We live in a world of worlds. And all of them ending. Flaming out. Collapsing.
Bernardo	We get everything wrong.
Candy	Yes, we do.
Bernardo	Just now I entered your living room with murder in my heart.
Candy	Me? Were you going to kill me?
Bernardo	I don't know why.
Candy	You thought my death would bring freedom.
Bernardo	Maybe.
Candy	Was it also sexual?
Bernardo	No. Does that hurt your feelings?
Candy	Not really.
Bernardo	I live without desire.
Candy	I don't believe you.
Bernardo	If you are a woman on this earth I am already inside of you.
Candy	No. You are *not* inside of me.
Bernardo	This is not the kind of argument you should want to win. I say this as your psychologist.
Candy	Men often think that kind of thing. Bud did before he went off to war. Oh, yes, he went to Baghdad. His hair got all burned off in Shock and Awe. It was just a start.

Of the work needing to be done. When he came home
from the V.A. That's when your friend John and I had
our conversation by phone. And I knew he would come
to me. If I bought enough clocks.

(*All the clocks stop at exactly the same time. A* CELLO
sounds, low. A pause. CANDY *resumes.*)

Candy   Bud's senses troubled him so we took steps. His eyes, his
ears. He couldn't talk because of the tongue. And the
brain thing with the needle behind the eyes. He had me
follow the instructions on line. And he was perfect then.
We went to see *Noah* with Russell Crowe. Me and Bud.
I left him in the multiplex. Naked, sightless. It's what he
wanted. And I left him knowing he would return as
something new, something higher, and reclaim his cap.
(*Then, holding out a bundle that has suddenly appeared
in her arms.*) Look, I've got this baby now.

(JOHN *comes alive—jumps up.*)

John   How can a man who has everything have nothing?! How
can a man who has everything have less than nothing?!
Hahahahaha!

Candy   (*At window.*) The hive is coming together again. Out of the
houses down from the buildings. We need each other now
to attain a reality basic. Only together can we become real.
And it's not a fascist thing. There is no leadership issue of.
But we all feel it. Being able to just... Know I don't. In
relax our own being. To just rest with each other a minute

for, an hour for... to rest. And be... quiet. And whole.
Moment for a words without... words without. Bud lead
the way all to that. And now... for you his cap is.

John   I don't want the cap.

Candy   Are you my buffalo? Are you my lynx?

John   I have this feeling if I put on Bud's stupid cap I will never
take it off again.

Candy   We are going to the caves now if you like.

John   I don't want the fucking cap... so why are my hands still
picking up the goddamn cap? Bernie?

Bernardo   Yes, boss.

John   Help me NOT put on this cap, Bernie. Bernie!

(BERNARDO *makes slow brick-laying motions with his
hands and body as* JOHN *wrestles against the impulse to
put on the cap.*)

Bernardo   I am lost in memories right now, boss. Building that sea
wall against the blue Caribbean. So that I can be free of
you, boss. No more, "Bernie, bring me a latte." "Bernie,
it's time to do yoga now." "Triangle pose, Bernie.
Triangle pose."

(JOHN *has put the cap on his head. The character named*
CANDY *will now be referred to as* CLARA.)

John   Are we in the cave now? I hear water dripping. Are we in
the cave? What's that? What's that sound?

(*A* CELLO *plays.*)

Clara	Not away far, the airport is. (CLARA *holds the baby to her breast*.)
John	We were off after the soldiers came. In our damaged truck. We came to the bar. I was drinking. I went to the men's room to wash my face. I want to ask you a question.
Clara	Is that what you came for?
John	Yes.
Clara	Is the question about a murder?
John	My neighbor in Belize. The guy owns titty bars in San Francisco. You remind me of someone, Candy.
Clara	Call me Clara now.
John	Clara, yes. That's who you remind me of. So I just hate this guy right from the start. We move in next to each other, right away the feuding begins. And then, I don't know, at a party on the beach we start talking, I think maybe he isn't so bad, this fat neighbor. And then I hate him even more because of the uncertainty. Maybe that's why I killed him. Do you hear sirens now?

(*A* CELLO *plays*.)

Clara	Do not any sirens hear I.
John	Uncertainty—I hate it. Always have. All kinds. What happened between you and me, Clara—that was the only real art, you know it was.
	(JOHN *looks at* CLARA. *She returns his gaze. More* CELLO.)
	What is this place anyway?
Clara	It's the cave where I just live now.

John	Oh did I mention I owe money? Debt, debt, debt. I'm in debt now. Kind of. How did you get younger? You're dead. We're both dead, is that it?
Clara	Here on stage we are.
John	Yes, I see that.
Clara	In the cave. Come closer and hello say.
John	(*To audience.*) Hello. (*Pause.*) Freaky. (*Pause.*) The stage is always the fucking bardo if you want my honest opinion. The bardo with trappings and banners.
Clara	Everywhere with banners and trappings the bardo is.
John	I'm not dead, I'm in fucking debt so I can't be dead. There's no magic in that. But all the animals are dying, that's for damn sure.
Clara	Would you like to baby hold?
John	Not in the least. I was supposed to be one of the heroes. What has happened? I owned *everything*.
Clara	He's your baby should you him hold.
John	My baby? How could he be my baby? That's insane.

(*CELLO as CLARA stands, cradling the baby…*)

Don't go…!

Clara	Go I won't.
John	I need you to stay near.
Clara	Effect caaaalming I have.
John	I killed a man last week, Clara. My photo is in all the papers.

(*Cello.*)

Clara	John?
John	Yeah?
Clara	What say you would?
John	What would I say if what?
Clara	(*Indicating audience.*) If see you they could.
John	Ah.
Clara	Could if see you them, what say you would?
John	What? Oh, I'd say "wait a minute." "What do you think this is?" Ha ha. No. (*Pause.*) I'd say... "*don't fuck with me.*" Or maybe I'd say... "*Look.*"
Clara	What look?
John	Just *look*, I don't know... Maybe that's what I'd say to myself. (*Pause.*) He was my neighbor... last Friday... I was very high... there were guns around...
Clara	And now done it is... done it is... done it is... done it—

(*The* cello *makes the sound of a siren, low, rising slowly in volume and then slowly receding again.* John *moves to the window and listens intently.*)

John	Now I'm here maybe I could borrow your baby. Just for the night.
Clara	(*To baby.*) When hold you I would... In your car or maybe in the park... Deepen, your breath began to deepen. I could feel it. Dying like an animal or being born.

294

John	My car, yes, my car, my car...
Clara	In my arms tiny you became baby again. Is how felt it... felt it... felt it... felt it... felt it... felt it—
John	And now of course a baby in my situation would come in very handy. You need money, people always do.

(CLARA *turns and looks at* JOHN. *He holds her gaze. The* CELLO *sounds.*)

Why is there a cello here?

Clara	A cello there's here because I like it.
John	(*To himself.*) Well that's a stupid reason.
Clara	The cello bees reminds me of. They're you know dying. The dying bees are. Maybe now you'd like to baby see your?
John	It's not my baby, Clara, OK?
Clara	You remember don't?
John	Remember what? The time you came to me and told me there would be a baby. And I said bullshit?

(CELLO-*siren fades away.*)

You lay on your side in the heat. You took pictures of yourself and sent them to me. You were naked, your body burning in the light.

Clara	You got off easy, man. I off let you easy.

(CLARA *moves close. As* JOHN *steps in to embrace her she hands him the baby in its blanket and steps away.* CELLO *low here throughout.*)

John   (*Holding the baby.*) Don't go. (*Pause.*) The words I said to you, Clara. Back when we had our—

Clara   On go.

John   I can't ever say those words again, I thought. To anyone else. Their meaning stayed with you, I thought. And now that you've gone...

(CLARA *steps back into shadow...*)

Clara   Sing didn't anyone teach you ever to?

(JOHN *turns to face front. Opens his mouth to sing. Falters, but then sings briefly, a tentative song.* CLARA *steps back out of the light, disappearing. The* CELLO *grows louder as lights slowly fade...*)

The End

Saint Simone

by Juli Crockett

Saint Simone *was presented by Padua Playwrights in a workshop reading at Robert Reynolds Art Studio and Gallery, Los Angeles, 2014, under the direction of the playwright, with the following cast:*

CHAD   *Gray Palmer*
DEREK   *Christopher Rivas*
THE SIMONE   *Caitlyn Conlin*

Characters

DEREK *and* CHAD   *Men in suits and ties.*
THE SIMONE   *A chorus of women.*

Setting

In **Excerpt One**, *an office. In* **Excerpt Two**, *the Court.*

Excerpt One

(CHAD *and* DEREK, *in suits and ties, are working out in their shared office space. They are using large books as free-weights and doing a ritualistic repetition of exercises, such as bicep curls, pushups, squats, lunges, and jumping jacks.*)

Chad Make a record of this. Hit record.

Derek (*Hits record.*) I'm recording.

Chad I shot a deer and I fucked it. It was still alive when I did it. It was looking back at me with its big brown doe eyes and I made full confession. Told it every awful thing I could think of that I'd done since the last deer I kill-fucked.

Derek Hunting season.

Chad It's good for the soul, confession.

Derek How much did you get for that deer?

Chad Not enough. Deer meat is worthless this time of year. I take it around to the poor huts and sell it cheap. Money ain't shit to me. It's the knowing that I came all up in that deer. That there's a piece of me in that meat, and all those disgusting grateful faces are gonna eat it up and take me in, swallow me like wafers at communion. That's how I get inside. And once I'm inside, I take over. Implanted. I commune up in there. Look at the map, all those dots moving around, all those people shuffling about, all of them me. I'm in them and I'm communicating with them. Your turn.

Derek I eat money. It tastes good. My lips get cut on the edges and it mixes with the blood. It hurts, like it should hurt, and when I shit, the coins rip my asshole and get stuck in the drain and I think, "This is what it is like to be a bank."

Chad   You better take your vitamins.

Derek   Vitamins are for people. I'm a bank. I'm a treasury. I'm a repository for riches. I am capital. I am the power of possessive thinking. I do my pushups. I endure the pain of Washington Jefferson Lincoln, Hamilton Jackson and Grant, Susan B. Anthony, Sacagawea, Franklin-McKinley-Cleveland, Madison-Chase-Woodrow-Wilson, pyramids and eyeballs and eagles and serial numbers and the signatures of the dead. My net worth is internal. Broken into tiny bits and decimals that no doctor can detect. Ink and paper in my blood. I am the printing press. I am an ATM. I've been doing this my whole life and you can't stop me.

Chad   My lunch got wet. I hate the rain.

Derek   I hate waiting.

Chad   Pretty much I hate everything. I hate until it's drained of its meaning. Hate becomes a preference. Hate becomes a sour taste, like rotten milk, in my mouth.

Derek   I like rotten milk. Unspoiled milk lacks character. No pizzazz.

Chad   I hate the word pizzazz.

Derek   I know. I hate myself for thinking it and even more for actually saying it. I hate my mind, language, the whole system.

Chad   The nervous system.

Derek   I hate being nervous.

Chad   I hate what's happening. What has happened and what is going to happen. I am consumed by hate. But we suck it up. We put on our big boy pants. We wait. We wait with my stupid wet lunch. We wait and I eat my stupid lunch and feed this eventual corpse: my body.

Derek   I hate my body.

Chad   I hate my body. I hate what is in it and what it is made of.

Derek   I hate those bitches.

Chad   We all hate them. Turn off the tape.

Derek   I want to destroy them.

Chad   We're gonna win. Don't worry. Turn off the tape.

Derek   I don't want to win, I want to destroy. I want to separate them and make them afraid. I want to smash their throats with ancient books and hear them wheezing.
I want them to apologize for ever having the fucking idea in the first place to raise their hand and speak.
I want them invisible. Never-been. I want them rewound into the womb and before, back into their father's balls. Un-done. Can we do that?

Chad   (*Turning off the tape.*) No. Not legally. No.

Derek   There are laws beyond the laws, and they are breaking those laws, I swear to god, and we should be breaking those laws right back. I swear to god.

Chad   There are other ways. There is divide and conquer. There is defamation of miracles. There is demolition of virginity. There is application of pain and the element of surprise, which will shock them to abandonment of the monotonous unity of their discourse. There is the individual assault.

Derek   We must pick them off one by one.

Chad   We're going to win.

Derek	Our job is to break them.
Chad	I love my job.
Derek	We could be excommunicated.
Chad	We don't have to sacrifice ourselves. We will speak abstractly. We will use statements that are open to interpretation and not admissible in court. We will frequently implement metaphors and obvious excess of euphemism. The crooked way is the best way. As the bird flies is unwise. Do you see what I'm saying? The little pigs, Goldilocks, the wicked witch, gnomes, dwarves, Billy goats, the bridge, the candy house, the oven, apple seeds, the national anthem, drag races, the abominable snowman, the superman, the comb over, x-ray vision, the undergarments, the needle in the haystack, the spider and the fly, do you follow? We must take the meandering path, and be sure to stop and chop the roses.
Derek	Yes, yes, yes.
Chad	Read to me from The Book. I need inspiration.
Derek	(He reads) Again, again, again, again, again, again, again, again, again, again, again, again, again, again, again, again, again....
Chad	Read on.
Derek	Against, against, against, against, against, against, against, against, against, against, against, against, against, against, against, against, against, against, against...
Chad	(*Overlapping.*) The candy house, the oven, the rabbit, the bricks, the flute, the oyster, the walrus, the carpenter, Jesus was a carpenter, if I were a carpenter. (*Flexes his*

	muscles.) We must think darkly. We must think thoughts in the dark. Turn out the lights.
Derek	(*Turns out the lights.*) Blackout. Disaster.
Chad	Yes, yes. That's much clearer. I can see now. My dark thoughts are lighter than the dark. But dark. Still dark. Finish the story.
Derek	(*Turns to the end of the book.*) He turned into a ball of light.
Chad	I open doors. I'm the opener. I am a highly trained professional. I get all of the most up-to-date memos. I know just which doors to open and when; therefore, and furthermore, that is why I'm the opener.
Derek	Should I open the door?
Chad	I will open the door. I am ready. I am ready to open the door.
Derek	I can smell them.
Chad	Arm yourself. Or don't. Release yourself. Infinitely.
Derek	Nothing is outside of God.
Chad	Everything is outside of God.
Derek	Nothing and Everything is outside of God.
Chad	There is no inside or outside of God.
Derek	No God. All God. I feel sick.
Chad	That's the hangover. Coming down. Positive. Think positive.
Derek	There are actually perfect moments. I know that now. I read it before, but now I know it.
Chad	Press record. (*DEREK hits record.*) You can open the door.
Derek	Thank you. Thank you. Thank you. (*DEREK tries to open the door, cannot. DEREK struggles with the door, becoming increasingly hysterical.*) Locked. Locked. The

door is locked. The door is locked. We are imprisoned. We are late. We are going to forfeit the game. We are going to lose. They are going to walk. They are going to walk all over us and grind our faces into the dirt. We are fools. We are nothing. We are in the wrong.

Chad It is not locked. It is jammed. This is why I am the opener. I shall open the door. (*CHAD performs a rehearsed series of knocks on the door frame, and the door opens with ease.*) We shall proceed.

*

Excerpt Two

(*THE SIMONE, a chorus of women speaking as one, addresses the court.*)

The Simone We who have devoted our bodies to the residence of She who was not what she seemed, We hereby speak with the tongue that gave forth the divine order of monotony, unaffected by joys and sorrows.

We, who have peered into the unveiled faceless glare of the great reality, stay true to the human incarnation vibratory pitch of forty-two octaves above middle C, vibrating 570 trillion times a second in ecstatic reverberation.

We, who have devoted our minds to the residence of She who was not what she thought or wrote, was or is, did or undid, carry on her divine task of breeding paradox (of the bob haircut and dark trench coat variety) pockets empty as the obedient heart expunged of all obstacles. Sucked dry, We, the devoted, bring forth the tormented mind occupied by the divine recurring migraine, holy migraine, said same migraine that inhabited the minds of the She that came before and before, divine migraine that transforms angels to demons revealing the interchangeability and the non-distinguishability of all things.

As similar at the atomic level as a violin and a rhinoceros (same) our father in heaven second cousin to the banana (same), closest relative to our DNA, We, the chosen, climb the tiny ladders and ascend beyond the limitations of origins.

No origin. No source. No priority. No pieces. No otherness. No mistakes.

We, upon the opening of the occupied mouth, pray for the mercy of She—relieve us of our idolatry and adolescence, show us our blindness and remove our vision so that we may see all you, all one, all in, in all things.

We, who represent the representation of a residence for the all-embracing resurrection of She:
    —She who spilled her soup *on purpose*
    —She who crushed her dainty fingers *on purpose*,
    —She who remained unwed *on purpose*,

—She who knew neither man nor woman nor animal nor mineral, nor silicone nor Styrofoam, *on purpose*,
—She who starved her heavenly body to death *on purpose*,
—She who failed her people on purpose, for all people, all purpose, for conflict for idiocy for hyperbole, for hypocrisy for ridicule and the deepest betrayal of source, for the source-less sorcery.

We, who have endured the privilege of the true vacuum, We do solemnly swear to tell the truth, the whole truth and nothing but the truth, so help your God.

The End

Forget Me That Way

by Guy Zimmerman

Forget Me That Way *was presented by S4 and Padua Playwrights at Elysian Valley Gateway Park in September of 2014, under the direction of the playwright, with the following cast:*

RICHARD   *Christopher Rivas*
GINA   *Lake Sharp*
LEECH   *Alex Brown*

Characters

RICHARD	*The spirit of a scientist.*
GINA	*The spirit of Richard's ex-wife, a former lab assistant.*
LEECH	*The spirit of Gina's lover.*

Setting

A park, ruined building or urban garden. Twilight.

(*Moving with ritualistic precision,* GINA, *face ghostly white, lays down a semi-circular line demarcating the playing area with white flour or chalk. Inside this arc she then draws two small circles—just large enough for a person to stand within. She retrieves a wooden stool from nearby and, carefully gauging hidden forces, places it carefully downstage of the two small circles. Immediately we hear conversational hubbub rising to a crescendo. Then steps.* RICHARD *enters, supported by* LEECH. *He wears a lab coat and one leg is completely stiff.* GINA *and* LEECH *step quickly into the two small circles and stand at attention, looking out. With exaggerated ceremony,* RICHARD *crosses and sits on the stool. He looks out at the audience for many moments, then gets out a small paper note pad and a pencil. He scribbles, rips a note off the pad, hands it to* GINA. *She reads the note.*)

Gina   (*Deciphering note.*) "On the day... of my execution... I was... cheerful."

(RICHARD *tears off a sheet of paper. Hands it to* LEECH.)

Leech   (*Deciphering note.*) "I was... charming... to the end."

(*A pause.* RICHARD *scribbles another note. Tears it off. Hands it to* GINA.)

Gina   (*Reading note.*) "Or so they tell me."

(RICHARD *hands note to* LEECH.)

Leech   (*Reading note.*) "Exterior, Elysian Valley Gateway Park, Frogtown—Night."

(RICHARD *hands note to* GINA.)

Gina   (*Reading note.*) "A man, Richard, forties, sits looking out... at a cloud of gentle..." (*She looks at audience.*) "... ghosts."

(RICHARD *hands note to* LEECH.)

Leech   (*Reading note.*) "With him... are the spirits... "
Gina   (*Reading note.*) "Of his ex-wife... and her lover... "
Leech   (*Reading note.*) "... a bearded... vegetarian."

(GINA *and* LEECH *smile, bow to the audience. A pause.*
RICHARD *scribbles another note. Tears it off. Hands it
to* GINA.)

Gina   (*Reading note.*) "With infinite nobility and charm he
opens his (*losing composure*) gaping, stinking mouth...
(*regaining composure*) to speak."

(RICHARD *glowers briefly. Smiles. He is opening his
mouth to speak when his right arm shoots straight up
into the air.* GINA *and* LEECH *move close. They pull the
sleeve of Richard's jacket down. There is writing on the
arm below. They read in turn.*)

Leech   (*Reading arm.*) "Have you ever... on your path through
this blinding world..."

Gina	(*Reading arm.*) "... had commerce... with a demon?"
Leech	(*Reading arm.*) "Have you ever been pursued?..."
Gina	(*Reading arm.*) "... were you offered riches, worldly power?"
Leech	(*Reading arm.*) "Did you weigh in the balance your standing among men?"

(*A pause.* RICHARD *drops his arm. Settles. Smiles. Abruptly he falls forward.* GINA *and* LEECH *glance at each other. Leech steps forward and raises the tail of Richard's lab coat . There is writing on Richard's back.*

Leech	(*Reading* RICHARD'S *back.*) "Dark falls the shadow... and in that darkness your own freedom!"
Gina	(*Reading* RICHARD'S *back.*) "I have burned in that fire! Flesh and bone I have been consumed!"
Leech	(*Reading back.*) "Some people believe in witches and ghouls!"
Gina	(*Reading back.*) "Beings of exceptional negativity!"
Leech	(*Reading back.*) "Afflicting the innocent!"
Gina	(*Reading back.*) "From hidden places!"
Leech	(*Reading back.*) "Sacred places!"
Gina	(*Reading back.*) "Obscure to the ordinary eye!"

(RICHARD *sits back up. Glowers. Smiles. Is about to get up to leave but stops and sits back down. Reaches into inside jacket pocket, pulls out a sandwich in wax paper, removes sandwich from wax paper, takes a bite. Chews*

slowly. Abruptly hands the rest of the sandwich to GINA.
*She takes it, holds it up, examines it closely, separates
the two slices of bread... and reads.*)

Gina   (*Reading sandwich.*) "All you ever wanted... dear
audience... was to secure happiness, avoid pain... you
were not 'bad'... Your children, certainly, they did not
deserve... the hideous diseases... "

(*Gina takes a bite of the sandwich. Hands the wax paper
to* RICHARD.)

Richard   (*Reading wax paper.*) "...and with viruses... I marked
their little hearts... gouging deep... (*looking up*) but then
I was the hunted one... (RICHARD *stands and quickly
steps out of the arc of the playing area.*) And yet—this is
what I had wanted all along! Ha ha ha ha ha ha...! To be
the hunted one...!"

(LEECH *and* GINA *look up. They see each other.*)

Gina   (*To* LEECH.) This ruined building is where he brought us
to die.

(*They look around with sudden recognition.*)

Leech   This is where we came... full of the poison.

(*They move and reach slowly toward each other and
embrace...*)

Richard   What are you doing?! Stop that! Stop what you are doing!

(GINA *and Leech turn to* RICHARD *and pause.*)

For God's sake, the past is the past...!

Gina   The past is *not* past...!

Richard   The past is dead and gone...!

Leech   No, the past lives on shaping what happens next...!

Richard   Even if that's true you're better off forgetting it...!

Leech   I can't forget it...!

(RICHARD *steps back into the circular playing area. He moves up behind* GINA *and* LEECH.)

Richard   (*To* LEECH.) When I met you... I knew... I would never see her again... EVERYTHING WAS FINE UNTIL YOU SHOWED UP!

Gina   (*To the audience.*) The criminal has been tried. The sentence has not yet been handed down.

Leech   (*To the audience.*) The crime has been committed. The punishment has not yet arrived.

Gina   (*To the audience.*) The time before the action...

Leech   (*To the audience.*) Stage time—re-enactments...

Gina   (*To the audience.*) Sacred time—first moment...

Leech   (*To the audience.*) Reenact the crime...

Gina   The crime was infection...

Leech   The cause of death a deadly pathogen...

Gina   (*To the audience.*) There's a little gas with the bloody stool, but I generally don't notice because of the projectile vomiting.

Leech	(*To the heavens.*) Let us have compassion for those who kill us.
Gina	(*To the heavens.*) Compassion for those who kill us is the only *true* compassion.

(*RICHARD paces in front now.*)

Richard	(*To audience, indicating* GINA.) "You're so alone," she said, "in your hideous laboratory," she said. "Your gene-splicing factory of death." She actually said those things to me. Long ago she said those hurtful things... (*To* GINA.) Does it not matter that I can see across a thousand years with my... Remarkable... Intelligence? (*To* LEECH.) And you—you were my brother...!
Gina	Oh, please, Richard...!
Leech	Stop trying to be better than everybody else...!
Gina	As if it would save you.
Leech	As if it were even possible.

(*RICHARD races back and sits.*)

Leech	(*To* GINA.) You made me so happy for a while.

(*GINA nods. Turns to audience.* RICHARD *rolls his eyes and gags throughout the exchange.*)

Gina	Look up and breathe.
Leech	We have no story.
Gina	There is no story that we are.

| Leech | We are only the world you see before you. |
| Gina | We are only the breath that moves through you. |

(RICHARD *stands and steps forward.*)

| Richard | Quick...! Some kind of sleazy action is called for...! (*Indicating audience.*) WHILE THEY ARE STILL WATCHING! |

(RICHARD *tries to get* GINA *and* LEECH *to copulate standing up.*)

Gina	They know what bodies are.
Leech	They know what bodies do.
Richard	But that's why I call them here. That's why I conjure them up. This cloud of happy ghosts...
Gina	No, let them go this time.
Leech	Let them fade away.
Gina	Let them forget they've always been here.
Leech	Let them imagine lives.
Richard	You could be happy. I could release you. Together you could be happy.

(*Pause.* GINA *and* LEECH *look at each other, as if tempted by* RICHARD'*s cryptic offer... then they sigh and turn again to the audience.*)

| Leech | (*To audience.*) We only come to say goodbye. But this goodbye will never leave you. |

Gina	(*To audience.*) Your end, when it comes toward you...
Leech	Galloping out of the light...
Gina	Well...
Leech	Who among us is prepared?
Richard	Demons...! (*A pause. He returns to stool. Smiles. Addresses audience.*) But demons always speak the truth: blood tastes like iron, you will find, as the world enters its new age of cinder and ash. Billions of years reel past, during which the seas rust and the sky burns white above the endless plains. The sun pours down its hot light and the planet spins in silence, a metal top. Perhaps even now it's not too late, you say to yourself. Yes, well, your lamentations were never pointless, never empty, but when I wake up you will forget who you are. (*He looks out at audience. Yawns.*) Well. Time to wake up.

(*RICHARD snaps his fingers. His head flies back. GINA and LEECH run forward two steps in a chaotic dance and freeze. Slowly they turn their torsos and look back at RICHARD. Freeze again. Lights gradually fade.*)

The End

This anthology is dedicated to all the actors who collaborated with the playwrights to bring these plays to life.

About the Playwrights

Sissy Boyd studied with Martha Graham and danced with many diverse and avant-garde companies in New York City. In Los Angeles, she studied poetry with Holly Prado, and playwrighting with John Steppling. Her play *Green Shoes* was directed by Wes Walker. Another play formed the text for a short film, *Liddy*, by Guy Zimmerman. Padua Playwrights Press includes *Liddy* in the anthology *Fever Dreams*. In 2006, Les Figues Press published Boyd's book *in the plain turn of the body make a sentence: 2 plays by Sissy Boyd*. She has danced in a myriad of Ken Roht's Orphean Circus theater creations. Her short plays have appeared in Kevin O'Sullivan's *Pharmacy* and Sharon Yablon's *Farm*.

Hank Bunker was born in Denver in 1961.

Juli Crockett is a bona fide renaissance woman: playwright, theater director, retired (undefeated) professional boxer and amateur champion, ordained minister, Doctor of Philosophy (*summa cum laude*), singer, songwriter, and leader of the genre-defying band The Evangenitals. Her work has been performed in New York, Los Angeles, Maine, and at the Edinburgh Fringe Festival. Her published works include *Void Creation: Theater and the Faith of Signifying Nothing* (Atropos Press) and *[or, the whale]* (Delere Press). She lives in Montecito Heights, California, with her husband, composer

Michael Feldman, their son Thelonious, and their pets: a tortoise named Mr. Turtle, and a cat named Žižek.

Heidi Darchuk is a writer and actor based in Los Angeles. In L.A., her plays have been commissioned/produced by Padua, Virginia Avenue Project and Pharmacy, as well as by A Contemporary theater and The Fringe Festival in Seattle. Her short fiction has been published by the Missouri Review (Audio Competition finalist) and Pontoon.

Bernard Goldberg teaches at West Los Angeles College, where he directed the Creative Writing Programs in Prague and Jerusalem. He was a member of John Steppling's Circus Minimus and Empire Red Lip; edited *Leighdt*, a New York City literary magazine; and published poems in *Lakeview International Journal of Literature and Arts*. He wrote and directed the short films *The Last Day* and *Cafe Morocco*, which won Honorable Mention at the 2013 Buffalo Niagara Film Festival.

Michael Hacker is a filmmaker and writer from Los Angeles. His first play, *Long Time Coming*, premiered at the Powerhouse Theater in Santa Monica in 1988. After attending the Padua Playwright's Festival and Workshop in 1991, Hacker focused more intently on theater, writing several works including *I Must Not Think Bad Thoughts (5 Short Plays)* and *Spoil*.

Susan Hayden's plays have been produced at The Met Theater, the Ruskin Group Theater, The Ensemble Studio Theater (Winterfest), the South Coast Repertory's Nexus Program, the Mark Taper Forum's Other Voices, Padua Playwrights, and Lost Studio. Her fiction has been widely published, and her poetry has appeared in *Hollywood Review*, *Arete*, and *Atlanta Journal*. She is the creator/producer of the monthly mixed-genre literary series "Library Girl." A collection of her poems will be published by Punk Hostage Press in 2015.

Coleman Hough is a poet, playwright, and screenwriter. Her poetry has appeared in many poetry journals including: *Southern Poetry Review*, *Alimentum* and *Cultural Weekly*. Her play, *Dressed for Dinner*, was produced by Padua Playwrights in a festival of short plays. *The Other Stories* (a trilogy of one acts) was workshopped at Circle in the Square theater in New York before being produced by Dixon Place. Her screenwriting credits include *Bubble* and *Full Frontal*.

Rachel Jendrzejewski is a playwright and performance artist. Her work has been developed and/or presented by Padua Playwrights, Playwrights' Horizons, The Wild Project, Institute of Contemporary Art/Boston, Rhode Island School of Design, Red Eye Theater, and the Walker Art Center, among others. She holds an MFA in Playwriting from Brown University. http://rachelka.com

Marc Jensen is a freelance writer and playwright living in Los Angeles. His plays have appeared in productions and staged readings by Gunfighter Nation and Padua Playwrights. His short story "Lotto Night" appeared in the literary journal *LA Miscellany*.

Christopher Kelley's plays have been produced in several places around L.A. since the '90s and in Austin and Chicago. He is a longtime collaborator with various Padua-related entities and is the recipient of several *LA Weekly* awards for plays produced at Theater of NOTE. This is his first published work.

Kevin O'Sullivan is a Los Angeles-based writer who, over the last two decades, has published research articles, obituaries, feature articles, and profiles in a variety of publications. He also conceived concepts for numerous music videos and has had several screenplays optioned. He has studied playwriting with both Murray Mednick and John Steppling. Since 2005 he has been the artistic director of Pharmacy, an occasional evening of short plays presented in non-traditional spaces.

Gray Palmer is a writer, composer, director and performer based in Los Angeles. He trained at Juilliard (Group VII) and HB Studio in New York City. He has been affiliated with Jean Erdman's Theater of the Open Eye (New York), Appaloosa Productions (Dallas), and since 2005 with Padua Playwrights. His plays for stage and radio have been presented by John Steppling's Gunfighter Nation, Padua Playwrights, Sharon's Farm, Pharmacy, and Machine Project.

Chris Rossi is a screenwriter, playwright and actor. He is the writer of the film *Meadowland* (2015), with Olivia Wilde, Luke Wilson, Elisabeth Moss, and Giovanni Ribisi, directed by Reed Morano. He has sold and developed film and television scripts, and his work has also been selected into Film Independent's Screenwriter and Directors Labs, as well as the No Borders film market in New York. He is a member of John Steppling's Gunfighter Nation workshop and has had his plays produced in Los Angeles.

April Rouveyrol is a Los Angeles-based playwright, director and screenwriter, born and raised in New York City. Her produced plays include *A Kink in the Release* (Heideman Award finalist,) *Night Jitters*, *What the Thunder Said*, and *Persons Unknown in a Room*

Above Sunset. She also produced, with Seth Landsberg, the cirque-electronica extravaganza *Ramayana 2K4* (Fabulous Monsters, La MaMa Theater, New York), which was nominated for five Drama Desk Awards, including Most Unique Theater Experience.

Cheryl Slean is a writer, filmmaker and educator exploring the intersection of the arts and sustainability. Recent theater work includes two site-specific commissions from Seattle University, and in L.A., *Plays at Pocket Park*, a pilot project of the Site-Specific Sustainability Series (S4), a proposed series of original plays and performances sited at provocative environments around Southern California, to help spark community interest and engagement in the promise of a sustainable future.

Wesley Walker's plays include *Wilfredo, The Conception,* and *Fully Formed Human Head.* His plays have been produced in Los Angeles by Bootleg Theater, the Echo Theater Company, the Lost Studio, Padua Playwrights, Theater of NOTE, Pharmacy and Sharon's Farm and have been published by Padua Playwrights Press and Doublewide Press.

Sharon Yablon writes, produces, sound-designs, and directs her own plays, and produces those by many others through Sharon's Farm. Her plays have been performed on KXLU and published in literary magazines and books, including *Desert Road's One Acts of Note* (2011). She was nominated for an *LA Weekly* Award in Playwriting. She is working on a short story collection set in Los Angeles and San Francisco; her first story, *Perfidia,* will be published by TAYO in December 2014.

A writer and director, **Guy Zimmerman** has served as the artistic director of Padua Playwrights in Los Angeles since 2001. Under his direction, Padua has staged more than thirty-five productions of new plays, moving several to venues in New York, Atlanta and abroad, and garnering a host of *LA Weekly*, Ovation, Garland, and Los Angeles Drama Critics Circle awards and nominations. As a playwright, his critically acclaimed work includes the plays *La Clarita, The Inside Job, Vagrant* and *The Black Glass*, which opened at the Ballhaus OST in Berlin in February of 2013. He is also the Supervising Editor of Padua Press, which has published six anthologies of new work by such nationally prominent playwrights as Maria Irene Fornes, Murray Mednick, John Steppling and John O'Keefe. His essays about film, theater, art and politics have appeared in *Theater Forum, LA Weekly, LA Theater Magazine*, the *LA Citizen*, and *Times Quotidian*, where he serves as Associate Editor. He is currently completing a doctoral degree in Drama and Theater at UC Irvine.

Padua Playwrights continues a writing, performance and teaching tradition that began Off-Off Broadway, and was sustained and refined at the Padua Hills Playwrights Workshop and Festival. Moving indoors since 2001, Padua has traded the immediacy of site-specific outdoor performances for the focus and finesse of an actual theater space. Continued though, has been the exploration of the spoken word and its myriad connections to the possibility of human meaning.

"**[Sharon's Farm]** has doggedly carried on a tradition of serious, home grown experimental play writing that has all but disappeared from the city's other stages..."   —Bill Raden, *LA Weekly*